OCCULT GRIMOIRE AND MAGICAL FORMULARY

OVER 500 SPELLS AND FORMULAS FOR LUCK, LOVE, PROSPERITY AND PEACE OF MIND

MARIA D'ANDREA

Global Communications

Occult Grimoire & Magical Formulary A Workbook For Creating A Positive Life

Occult Grimoire & Magical Formulary
Over 500 Spells and Formulas For Luck, Love, Prosperity and Peace of Mind

BY MARIA D' ANDREA

This revised edition and new cover art
Copyright © 2012
Timothy Green Beckley
DBA Global Communications, All Rights Reserved
Copyright ©1990 by Maria V. D'Andrea
Copyright ©2002 – Revised. By Maria V. D'Andrea.

EAN: 978-1-60611-108-6
ISBN: 1-60611-108-6

No part of this book may be reproduced, stored in retrieval system or transmitted in any form or by any means, electronic, mechanical, photocopying, recording, without express permission of the publisher.

Timothy Green Beckley: Editorial Director
Carol Rodriguez: Publishers Assistant
Sean Casteel: Associate Editor
Cover Art: Tim Swartz
Art Work by Mark Taylor

Printed in the United States of America
For free catalog write:
Global Communications
P.O. Box 753
New Brunswick, NJ 08903

Free Subscription to Conspiracy Journal E-Mail Newsletter
www.conspiracyjournal.com

DEDICATION

To my spiritual children:

>Rob D'Andrea, for his entrepreneur abilities and drive.
>Rick Holecek, for his spirituality and connection to nature.
>Gina Holecek, Rick's wife and now my daughter, for her sincerity and upbeat attitude.

To my mother, Maria Berde, a woman of vision held back only by reality.

To my friend, Cheryl Schaeffer, who has helped me to travel back so that this book could be reborn.

I wish to express my appreciation for the help, belief and enthusiasm for this book to; Francis Revels-Bey – my Spiritual Brother, Robert Krachenfels and Mark Taylor.

May they always stay Light Workers.

Information and formulae contained within these pages are meant only as suggestions. Derived from traditions and practical use within our higher circle of Mystics.

Special thanks to my son, Robert D'Andrea for his help and patience in the production of this book.

Occult Grimoire & Magical Formulary A Workbook For Creating A Positive Life

INTRODUCTION

This book has been written to help you achieve the power to create a better life for yourself with the help of Spiritual tools. You can do it! The author, Maria Solomon, is a talented psychic practitioner who has worked with thousands world wide to help them achieve that which they desired. She proclaims:

"The art of metaphysics is a very ancient one. Metaphysics in the dictionary is described in the following manner: 'The science which investigates first causes of all existence and knowledge.' Occult is described as: 'The doctrine or study of the supernatural, magical, etc.'

"As can be seen from this, we are dealing with a form of art and science. Much of the ancient knowledge has been lost to us since it was passed down largely by word of mouth, in secrecy. Even in some books, a portion of the formula is left out, written in code, or in a style in which it is taken for granted that you already have an understanding of the field.

"This is understandable when you realize how much power and control is being taught. You can control the elements of nature when you comprehend the process of how to do it. You must always remember that the elements of nature are neutral - neither positive or negative. You as the practitioner are positive or negative, thus putting it to your own use.

"Only a few metaphysical books are written to the universal reader. This book contains only positive works, as we are all meant to be working on the Path of Light.

"We are meant to work on a balance consisting of spiritual and physical. We need to attract into our lives that which we need and want to be happy. We are working from spirit, but in a physical body with its own needs. After all, it is difficult to work from spirit when all your energy is spent on acquiring food. It is also just as difficult to hold onto a major amount of money if you do not acknowledge the source as being Divine Power. For us to be happy, we need to work from both the spiritual and physical realms.

"Use the higher knowledge contained in this book only with positive intentions. You will be amazed at how that which you require the most will come to you. We are but a tool through which Divine Power manifests to attract our needs and wants."

Occult Grimoire & Magical Formulary A Workbook For Creating A Positive Life

Table of Contents

CHAPTER ONE — *- 13 -*

MANIFESTING YOUR FUTURE — - 13 -
- meditation — - 17 -
- correspondence of magic and astrology — - 27 -
- planetary activities — - 29 -

CHAPTER TWO — *- 31 -*

PSYCHIC SELF DEFENSE — - 31 -
- Signs of attack — - 35 -
- the shield of protection — - 36 -
- spiritual bath formula — - 42 -

CHAPTER THREE — *-45 -*

HERBAL MAGNETS — - 45 -
- love — - 48 -
- money — - 49 -
- luck — - 49 -
- court — - 50 -
- job — - 50 -
- love spells — - 50 -
  - love charm — - 51 -
  - passion — - 52 -
  - to break a love spell — - 53 -
  - to attract new friends — - 53 -
- money attractions — - 54 -
  - gambling — - 54 -
  - wealth — - 55 -
  - money drawing bag — - 55 -
  - bringing in money on a power level — - 55 -
  - to find money — - 57 -
  - to draw money — - 57 -
  - nest eggs — - 57 -
  - attract riches into your home — - 58 -
- court — - 58 -
  - to win a case — - 58 -
  - for court — - 59 -
  - to carry into court — - 59 -
  - infusion — - 59 -
- protection — - 59 -
  - protection from illness — - 60 -
  - baths for protection and cleansing — - 60 -
  - to protect your family — - 61 -
  - home protection — - 62 -
  - protection from negative spirits — - 62 -
  - protection from curses — - 62 -
  - protection of your house while you are away — - 63 -
  - get rid of evil - to be safe — - 64 -
  - to change vibrations — - 64 -
- prophetic dreams — - 64 -

- 7 -

Occult Grimoire & Magical Formulary A Workbook For Creating A Positive Life

CHAPTER FOUR — *- 67 -*

TREASURE MAPPING — - 67 -
- creating your map — - 72 -
- affirmations — - 77 -

CHAPTER FIVE — *- 83 -*

RITUAL OILS — - 83 -
- For magical Work — - 86 -
- magnetic oil — - 87 -
- love attraction — - 87 -
- love oils — - 87 -
- magnetic oil for psychic powers — - 88 -
- success — - 88 -
- hex-breaking — - 88 -
- happiness — - 89 -
- lucky life — - 89 -
- love — - 89 -
- love attraction — - 91 -
- magnetic Oil to attract men — - 91 -
- magnetic oil to attract women — - 91 -
- energy — - 92 -
- psychic ability — - 92 -
- house cleaning — - 92 -
- study — - 93 -
- attract friends — - 93 -
- money — - 93 -
- sleep — - 94 -
- power — - 94 -
- fast money — - 95 -
- new home — - 95 -
- peace at work — - 96 -
- mental power — - 97 -
- money magnet — - 97 -
- medicine bag for love attraction — - 99 -
- a note on cutting the oils — - 99 -

CHAPTER SIX — *- 102 -*

CANDLE MAGIC — - 102 -
- candle types and attractions — - 106 -
- candle colors — - 108 -
- astral colors — - 110 -
- astrology signs — - 111 -
- color vibrational connection — - 111 -
  - astral candles — - 111 -
- day and places — - 113 -
- planetary days and hours - activities — - 114 -
- timing of rituals — - 116 -
- your personal day for candleburning — - 117 -
- personal day — - 119 -
- fixing the candle — - 123 -
- candle formulae — - 124 -
  - Unhexing — - 126 -
  - prophecy — - 126 -

Occult Grimoire & Magical Formulary A Workbook For Creating A Positive Life

wishes	- 126 -
to overcome an enemy	- 127 -
love	- 127 -
new love	- 127 -
love attraction	- 128 -
love spell	- 128 -
bring money in	- 129 -
to win in court	- 129 -
improving business	- 130 -
spirituality	- 130 -
financial gain	- 131 -
success	- 131 -
obtaining money	- 132 -
overcome obstacles	- 134 -
happiness	- 134 -
luck	- 134 -

CHAPTER SEVEN — *137* —

UNLOCKING THE SECRETS OF LOVE POTIONS — - 137 -

hypocras aphrodisiaque	- 141 -
elfin spirits	- 141 -
syrup of priapus	- 142 -
liqueur of love	- 142 -
sweet passion	- 143 -
tiger lust	- 143 -
eye of the giant	- 145 -
gentian wine	- 145 -
dragon wine	- 146 -
sexual power	- 146 -
wine of the wizard	- 147 -
wine of the sword	- 147 -
sword of power	- 147 -
goblin juice	- 148 -

CHAPTER EIGHT — *150* —

MYSTICAL INCENSE — - 150 -

vibrational influences	- 153 -
incense formulae	- 157 -
for concentration	- 157 -
quieting effect	- 159 -
heaviest cleansing method	- 159 -
fast money	- 159 -
finance	- 159 -
un-hex	- 159 -
love	- 160 -
positive home	- 160 -
fast business	- 161 -
formulae to get a new job	- 162 -
magnet attractions	- 162 -
spirit helpers	- 162 -
psychic vibrations	- 163 -
protection	- 163 -
to increase opportunity	- 163 -
harmony	- 163 -

Occult Grimoire & Magical Formulary A Workbook For Creating A Positive Life

- prophecy — 164 -
- seeking spirit aid — 164 -
- to attract love — 165 -
- finance — 165 -
- court — 166 -
- raise and job promotion — 166 -
- cleanse home — 167 -
- lost objects — 167 -
- smudging — 168 -

CHAPTER NINE — 169 -

CRYSTALS AND STONES A SOURCE OF POWER — 169 -

CRYSTALS AND STONES A SOURCE OF POWER — 171 -

- cleansing the stones — 174 -
- help in meditation — 175 -
- meditation aid — 175 -
- love attraction — 176 -
- infidelity — 176 -
- love - very powerful — 177 -
- health — 177 -
- money attraction — 177 -
- to fulfill any wish — 178 -
- to remove tension — 178 -
- to bring in courage — 180 -
- leadership ability — 180 -
- money attraction — 180 -
- success — 180 -
- spirituality — 181 -
- health — 181 -
- to not be controlled — 181 -
- high luck — 181 -
- protection — 182 -
- intellect — 182 -
- dreams — 183 -
- harmony — 183 -
- weather magic — 184 -
- energy — 184 -
- sincerity — 186 -
- relieve depression — 186 -
- love — 186 -
- money drawing — 187 -

CHAPTER TEN — 189 -

PRAYER — 189 -

- psalms — 193 -
  - to come to you — 193 -
  - for help — 194 -
  - prayer for help — 194 -
  - for legal matters — 194 -
  - to protect your home — 194 -
  - overcome enemies — 195 -
  - business to grow — 195 -
  - protection from people who mean you harm — 195 -

when you are depressed	- 195 -
thanks for prayers answered	- 195 -
psychic ability strengthened	- 196 -
spirituality	- 196 -
to be safe during travel	- 196 -
love attraction	- 196 -
when faced with problems	- 196 -
love	- 197 -
increase of crops	- 197 -
deliverance from persecutors	- 197 -
to be blessed	- 197 -
for a harmonious family	- 197 -
money attraction	- 198 -
luck	- 198 -
protection from enemies	- 198 -
petition	- 198 -
turn your luck around	- 198 -
to praise god	- 199 -
help in times of trouble	- 199 -
bring us joy	- 199 -
clearing of confusion	- 199 -
love attractions	- 200 -
attract good business	- 200 -
wisdom	- 200 -
to bring in help when needed	- 200 -
to focus on a positive future	- 200 -
affirmations	- 201 -
occult law of indifference	- 204 -
affirmations to counteract	- 206 -
protection prayer	- 211 -
wishes fulfilled	- 214 -
your own prayer	- 214 -
conclusion	- 215 -
QUIZ	**- 218 -**
PRAYER FOR POWER	**- 227 -**
OTHER BOOKS BY MARIA D'ANDREA	**- 233 -**
FOR ADDITIONAL INFORMATION	**- 234 -**

Occult Grimoire & Magical Formulary A Workbook For Creating A Positive Life

CHAPTER ONE

MANIFESTING YOUR FUTURE

MANIFESTING YOUR FUTURE

This is a practical guide to those traveling the Path of Light.

Have you ever noticed how some people always have everything they desire in life? They have a good relationship, financial security, success in business, and in all aspects of life; while other people seem always to have things going wrong. Do you ever wish your life could improve?

Now is the time to make that very important change come about. God wants us to be happy and to prosper. He did not say, "I want you to have *some things*, but not money, etc." The Bible said in Psalm 23:1, "The Lord is my shepherd; I shall not want." And in Psalm 122:7, "Peace be within thy walls, and prosperity within thy palaces." He wants us to be happy on ALL levels. How can you be happy when you do not have enough money for food? Or if you are tense or feel frustrated with the path your life is taking?

The power of the word has been known throughout the ages. When we make an affirmation through Divine Power, knowing it will come to pass, it *does* manifest. Realize that you have infinite supply through Divine Intelligence.

Anything positive or good that you want can come into your life. You have to change your outlook first. If you think "poor", that is what you will attract. If you think "rich", then that will be attracted to you. The power of the word is very real. It influences your subconscious, your actions, and the astral and physical planes.

First, see in your mind what you want in as much detail as possible. Concentrate upon it. Feel it. Know within yourself that it will happen. Out loud or to yourself express your desire as a positive affirmation, such as: I am God's child and He will take care of all of my needs. Always add:

1. *Through Divine Power.* You are saying everything comes from God.

2. *In A Perfect Way.* What you want will happen in a positive way, not harming others. As an example: If you see a house you love and you desire that house, you will get it. If you do not say, "In A Perfect Way," however, you may get it due to impending bankruptcy of the owners, necessitating their having to sell the house quickly, at a low price. Then you might get the house because they had a better job offer in a distant area. Then they would want to move and would still sell fast at a low price.

3. *I Want This Or Something Better.* You want to make sure that if you cannot have exactly what you want, you will get something that is equal to it. If you do not say, "Or Something Better," you might be closing off an opportunity to do better, thus putting a limit on yourself.

4. *Thank God.* As if what you want has already come to pass. Matthew 7:7 states, "Ask and it shall be given you, seek and ye shall find, knock and is shall be opened unto you." The Bible does not say *maybe*, it says "*shall* be."

This works on all levels. You might need a new job, a new or better relationship, or improved health.

Words and thoughts form our lives. You have to *relax* and spend 15-20 minutes each day *concentrating* on what you desire, *knowing* that it will come true. In Matthew 9:29 we find the words, "According to your faith be it unto you." In essence, what you expect from life will be what you get. *Expect* good. *Expect* prosperity.

Allow yourself to be interested in those around you. Be happy and let others see that you care. Don't dwell on your past, but think of all the good that will come in your future. Be receptive to God and the Spiritual Law. It is like being a magnet. You attract what you want; repel what you do not.

Work with the Spiritual Law. If you have a situation in your life that is negative, do not fight it. Concentrating on it gives it power. Relax and leave it in the hands of God. It will be taken care of.

We are all part of God. You have to act in a positive way. Use the Power of the Word. Know that you will receive what you ask for. Remember at all times, "All things whatsoever ye ask in prayer, believing, ye shall receive."

MEDITATION

Meditation is one of the most well-known, but least understood, methods of achieving self-awareness. People all over the world have tried various forms of meditation, but few actually understand it. From books written on the subject, to traveling to remote places in India, people have tried to gain this knowledge.

While there are people working diligently on achieving it, at times they miss the concept -- that the aim of meditation is to relax and get in touch with the Godhead that is within each of us.

This state of relaxation cannot be forced or coerced. It comes when you leave yourself open, when your guard is down, and your attitude is one of quiet waiting. For some people it may come after a few tries, but for most it takes a longer period of time, depending on your level of consciousness. It may be "active" or "passive," active meaning that you meditate wherever you are, aware of your physical self, whereas passive meditation is accomplished when you are in private.

It is said that one objective of meditation is to know yourself. While this may not be necessary, it is always to your advantage to know who you actually are. Not where you are or your name or your physical appearance, not even your sociological relationship with other people, but to know who you are in relation to yourself and the cosmic forces. Though now always sought after, it is an important side result of meditation. You're open to the Universal Mind -- the Cosmic Energy -- the Godhead. Your openness and calm alertness draw to you that which is essential to your happiness and well-being. It is like being on a river bank with a waiting net. You perceive what flows by; what you need or can use, you will acquire. What is non-essential you will let flow past.

The Godhead, being impartial, will invariably let pass before your inner mind scenes of past, present and future. If you learn to "see" and pay attention to your intuitive senses, you will learn how to cope better with life, avoid some pitfalls and know which areas are most in need of help.

You can control your energies so as to not drain them uselessly, conserving on movements that waste your life force. When you don't know how to be "still" within yourself, you waste your energy and your time. With practice, you will be able to accomplish what you must with a minimum of effort.

You will need to practice every day for at least twenty minutes. Four times a week is considered minimum in some circles. Others say that the best times to meditate are at sunrise and sunset, half an hour before breakfast, half an hour after dinner. Actually there is really no right or wrong time of the day in which you can meditate. You choose the time that works best for you.

Meditation can help you have a more abundant and happy life. You have more control over your life, not being buffeted by the whims of circumstance. Remember there are many forms of meditation. If you don't feel comfortable with one form, try other methods until you find the ideal one for you. Whatever form you select will be a personal matter.

I sincerely recommend that you try meditation. It will help you to receive the benefits of life that are yours to claim.

My personal method is very simple and direct. It took about 15 years of hit-and-miss trials before I conceived it. When I teach Psychic Development classes, I find that everyone can utilize my method. It always works!

I discovered that the trouble with using some of the other methods was that the focus was placed outwardly rather than inwardly. It will not work when you are told to look at a candle flame and focus on it; to listen to music (which *does* work before meditation); on water, or on any outward focus. These methods are really concentration.

To meditate you need to go inward instead, to let go. Anything outward keeps your focus on this reality instead of the alpha reality. You can't do both at the same time in meditation. It is best not to meditate for more than 15 to 30 minutes at one time. After that time, we start refocusing on this reality or daydreams may start.

First, close your eyes. Make sure your spine and head are aligned. Lie down on something comfortable or sit in a comfortable chair with your feet elevated, such as on a pillow. This keeps you from being grounded. Think of it as being a lightning rod. You don't want the energy to pass back through you to the earth. (If you are somewhere that makes it inconvenient, you can still meditate.) I want you to work with full force here. Never cross your arms or your legs. You would be blocking the energy flow.

Relax your body. Use progressive relaxation in the beginning. Later, as you become used to relaxing, your body will do so automatically.

Do the following progressive relaxation exercises, starting with your feet:

Toes

Arches of feet

Rising to ankles

To knees

To thighs and hips

Rising up the spine

To neck and shoulders

Moving downward to the upper arms, to the forearms

To wrists, hands and fingers

Back up the arms to the shoulders

Then moving downward through the chest and stomach

Again moving upward to the neck (making it loose and limp)

Allowing that relaxation to move to the scalp

Moving over forehead and brow (relaxing as it goes)

Down to the eyes

Now squeeze the eyes as hard as you can

Now relax them and feel all the peacefulness and relaxing power flow over them

Allow that relaxation to move to the cheeks and jaw

Now allow a small space between your teeth so that your jaw can remain slack.

Feel happy. Don't think negative thoughts at this time.

Say the following affirmation to yourself:

The Lord is in His Holy temple. Let there be peace, peace, peace.

You are simply affirming where your information is coming from -- Divine source.

Next, I want you to do abdominal breathing. This will calm you emotionally. After all, it is difficult to relax fully when your emotions are in turmoil. It will also help you go down levels into yourself. To do this:

Breathe in, and as you do, have your stomach go out.

Breathe out, pull your stomach in.

Do this breathing for three or four minutes. Then with each breath count backward from ten to one. By one, you should have a euphoric feeling. Place your attention in front and a little above you. Visualize a white to golden white screen. Any screen - TV, movie, etc. I personally visualize the screen that is at a drive-in movie. It's big. I find if I use a television screen, I end up adding channel selectors. If I use the movie screen, I end up adding the seats in the front. Use whichever one works the best for you. If you get a void or blackness, that's all right. Leave it. If you force the white color too much, you will refocus back to this reality.

Next, say something to yourself to let your subconscious know you are ready, such as: I want to start now, I am ready.

You will start seeing your thoughts and psychic information coming through. It doesn't always come in fast. Sometimes there are periods of time between visions. Do not rush it. Relax.

You may see something pertaining to your everyday problems, bills, etc. Don't feel you are not meditating. You are. Look at the information. You may be getting a solution or perhaps putting things into perspective, such as the point of view of your boss, which you didn't understand previously. You may get information about your future or some other message.

When you are ready to end your meditation session, you need to CLOSE YOUR CHAKRA. This is a very important last step! When you are meditating, you are very open on a psychic level. You need to shut down. Otherwise, it is as though you are walking around with your nerve endings raw. You will be sensitive and hurt emotionally very easily.

To close your chakra, extend your arms to shoulder level, palms facing front. Then bring them in, crossing them in front of your chest. Next, cross your legs. You are pulling your aura into yourself. Your aura extends more during meditation.

Do not get up fast. Remember your muscles were fully relaxed.

You may want to set a kitchen timer in the beginning so you will not have an urge to look at the clock and thus ground yourself. Give yourself a few extra minutes with the timer. It will take some extra time to relax at first. After you become accustomed to going down to your psychic levels, this will occur much faster.

Give yourself a code word to help it along. After you have been doing the progressive relaxation for a span of time, you will find it becomes easier. When this happens, give yourself a code word before you start the relaxation -- any word that you find connects for you, such as: Relax; Now; Ready. You are now programming your subconscious to know that when you use the code word, this is the process you expect to happen. You will be able to physically relax and go limp instantly.

The same procedure can be used for the breathing technique. You will be able to drop into your relaxed, calm and deep emotional levels immediately upon saying your code word.

You can also use these methods in other situations in your life. You may be under stress at work. Yet there may not be a place or the time to go somewhere to meditate. You can still utilize this technique to relax physically. When you are under stress your muscles tighten. You may choose to relax emotionally.

There are levels of awareness that we can consciously put to use. Our normal, everyday brain wave level is called Beta. Alpha and Theta are the levels in which psychic occurrences take place. One level above Alpha and Theta is known as Delta. These are altered states of awareness.

It is as though you are capable of seeing two realities, both equally real. One is our own material reality, the other is the Alpha reality. It is merely the ability to tune in.

The average person only uses ten percent of his potential. With your brain wave on Alpha, you can heighten this level and put it to more positive uses, helping yourself and others.

First you need to learn how to relax your body and mind. Sensory impulses must be blocked out, allowing you to develop your subconscious and super-awareness.

You need to block out your mental thought process. You cannot do two things at the same time. If you are using mental thought, you will be unable to reach the deeper levels within yourself. For example, you cannot achieve a relaxed state if your legs are cramped, since your thoughts will then be centered on your discomfort.

One of the most effective ways to tune into Alpha is to meditate. First visualize and feel yourself inside each color of the rainbow -- Red, Orange, Yellow, Green, Blue, Violet. With each color go deeper into yourself. Then slowly count backward from twenty to one, feeling more and more relaxed and going deeper into yourself. When you get to one, visualize a door in front of you. Go through it and into a comfortable room with a big white screen. Here is where you will see what is in your past, present and future. If you need to solve a problem, as an example, you would put the problem on the screen, and give it a little time to show you a solution. The answer will come to you.

There is the Infinity of the Universe in all of us, and so we are all connected, tuned in. When you go down into your deeper levels, you acquire the ability to create, heal, understand, etc. If you want to reorganize your negative habits, you visualize it in a positive way on your screen. Your subconscious sees both as reality. (Beta and Alpha.) It also takes everything literally. Through visualization and meditation, it will accept your input, and change your outward life. Your body and consciousness will respond promptly.

We are responsible for our thoughts which cause these changes. Remember, "Ask and ye shall receive, seek and ye shall find, knock and the door shall be opened." This is a very real way of working with your life.

At the Alpha level, problems are solved after your consciousness says, "I give up. Help!" It balances your physically, mentally and emotionally. It is a positive way to acquire what you want or need and to help others.

As Emerson said, "Be careful of what you wish for, or you may get it." With practice, you will go into the Alpha level faster. Work with it and be constructive.

One of the reasons we can attract that which we need is because of the fact that everything has vibrations or energies. Scientifically these energies have been tested. One such test is known as Kirlian photography. This is a camera, used by some psychics to do readings, which takes a picture of your vibrations. Animate and inanimate objects all have their own energies. These vibrations can be put to use attracting our desires. The fact that we are working through Divine Power is enough to attract all our needs.

There are certain considerations when you work which also add power and high energy levels.

CORRESPONDENCE OF MAGIC AND ASTROLOGY

Though not essential, perform ceremonies on the day in the hour of the correct planet. Each day and hour has its planetary ruler:

Sunday	Ruled by the Sun
Monday	Ruled by the Moon
Tuesday	Ruled by Mars
Wednesday	Ruled by Mercury
Thursday	Ruled by Jupiter
Friday	Ruled by Venus
Saturday	Ruled by Saturn

The planet that rules the day also rules the first hour after sunrise of that same day, and the hours after that are ruled by the following planets in this order:

1 - Sun
2 - Venus
3 - Mercury
4 - Moon
5 - Saturn
6 - Jupiter
7 - Mars

Occult Grimoire & Magical Formulary A Workbook For Creating A Positive Life

At sunset the hours begin again. The first hour after sunset is ruled by the planet which comes fifth in order from the planet that rules the day.

Example:

	Thursday (Day of Jupiter)	Friday (Day of Venus)
First hour after sunrise	Jupiter	Venus
Second hour after sunrise	Mars	Mercury
Third hour after sunrise	Sun	Moon
Etc.		
First hour after sunset	Moon	Mars
Second hour after sunset	Saturn	Moon
Third hour after sunset	Jupiter	Venus
Etc.		

The following sunrise introduces the start of a new day. Thus each planet rules the 1st and 8th hours of daylight; the 3rd and 10th hours of the night on its own day.

PLANETARY ACTIVITIES

Sun: Gaining favor; friends; wealth; healing; good fortune; operations concerning employers; promotions.

Moon: Love; messages; travel; emotions; medicine; dreams.

Mercury: Study; fast luck; quick money; business; divination; Spiritual work; to lift hexes.

Venus: Making friends; travel; love; fertility; art.

Mars: Energy; passion; war (offense and defense).

Jupiter: Preserving health; gaining riches; obtaining honors; legalities; court success.

Saturn: Causing good or bad fortune to business; learning; destruction; gaining possessions; spiritual work for protection; legalities for family; lift negativity and protect from enemies.

Intention is really the most important factor. If the energies are there and you recognize your source as Divine Power, then nothing else matters.

Magic is a science of nature with its own laws, so to be safe, stay positive with your intentions.

Never harm anyone, as it will come back to you threefold. Threefold comes back from any work, positive or negative. Negative magic is never worth the penalty that must be paid.

Metaphysical work does not have an exact time span. Some can work quickly, some may take continuous work to get results. After all, the pyramids didn't take but a day to build, either. The results were worth the wait.

Think of attracting your needs metaphysically as a triangle.

1. You put forth the thought or word of what you want.

2. The thought goes to the higher realm of the astral plane and forces go to work to manifest your needs.

3. It comes back down to the material plane and forms on the material level.

This does not mean we must be serious and not joyous. Simply be aware of that which you put into motion.

CHAPTER TWO

PSYCHIC SELF DEFENSE

Occult Grimoire & Magical Formulary A Workbook For Creating A Positive Life

PSYCHIC SELF-DEFENSE

Psychic defense is extremely important when you are working with metaphysics since you are being very open on a psychic level. Hence, it needs to be learned and utilized prior to any "work".

I feel that knowledge of psychic self-defense and meditation is a priority. These are the foundations upon which to build. Once you know how to use both, you can do anything.

There are many misconceptions concerning the definition of a psychic attack. Factually, it is a conscious or subconscious pouring forth of negative vibrations or thoughts from one or more persons to another.

If someone is jealous of your opportunity for a job promotion, this person is sending negative energy, whether on purpose or not. It could cancel out your opportunity or the level of it coming in.

Everyone needs psychic self-defense. It is a necessity for mystics, occult practitioners, creative people, and free thinkers as a protection against jealousy on a professional level, or disbelievers who may cancel them out.

Psychics, sensitive and/or emotional people are very open to vibrations on a sensitive level.

Business people and successful people in all walks of life may have rivals who do not want them to succeed in their endeavors.

Clergy, those working in hospitals (especially mental hospitals), counselors, police, anyone dealing directly with groups of people, must practice psychic self-defense.

Depression, hostility, confusion, and all forms of negativity can be transmitted in a psychic attack.

People who are ill must conserve their strength in order to regain their health. Unseen influences attach to weakness.

Most arguments are within the family and/or with relatives.

People who are at home may be confronted by pushy salespeople and neighbors who drain them.

Children are very open to suggestion, such as backward masking (music played backward with a negative message).

The defense is due to our energy fields, our auras being frequently under attack. Everyone has this energy field. It is very real, and can be visual. Kirlian photography allows one to take a picture of this aura. There are different auric layers, the main two being the physical aura and psychic aura.

The physical aura surrounds the physical body and this is where health may be seen. It has a dull glow.

The psychic aura surrounds the astral body (your energy body). The psychic attack is felt here first. This aura has many bright colors.

The attacker is called a Psychic Vampire, an energy thief who may be a spirit entity or a living being, people in our daily life.

Generally, these attackers fall into the following categories:

Elemental - nature spirit. May be a negative one.

Earthbound Spirits - spirits on a low spiritual level. These are energy thieves who drain us physically and emotionally, much as a flashlight drains a battery (us). There are also those who are living through people, such as alcoholics, drug addicts, gamblers, etc.

Ghosts - those who are seeking help in crossing over, or looking for a solution to a problem that existed in a previous life.

Demons - demonic possession, a rare occurrence.

There are also those people on our plane who do not use their own energies well so they steal yours, i.e., people who call you on the phone ten times during a day, leaving you drained. Those who hold a great deal of negativity may hurl psychic barbs at you because of resentment, jealousy, possessiveness - an example is the *Evil Eye*.

SIGNS OF ATTACK

The first signs of psychic attack begin on the psychic level, then may turn physical. These are symptoms of psychic attack only when they are unusual for you. If you normally have frequent headaches, then it is not caused by this. If you never have headaches and then they become constant, check the cause. Other symptoms might be:

Sleeplessness or fitful dreams
Headaches
Stomach cramps

Short, fast breathes

A pain that is felt in the weakest part of the body

Unfocused vision

Depression

Personality change

Anger

Lack of energy

Lack of patience

What you are really defending is your aura. Everything manifests in your aura first, then physically, mentally or emotionally.

Your aura can keep entities out unless you give them permission to enter. It will also tone down the negativity in your environment. If people argue at your job constantly, you will still be aware of it, but it will not bother you as much. It may actually stop the quarrels when you are there. One of the strongest methods of protection is as follows:

THE SHIELD OF PROTECTION

The first time do this standing up to get the feel of it.

Stand with your hands down at your sides

Visualize White Light pouring down from about one foot above your head, an umbrella effect.

Visualize it coming down on all sides of you to about one foot below your feet.

Visualize yourself as being in the center of the white egg-shaped sphere. As you do so, say:

> I am now putting up God's Shield of White Light,
> of Love, Truth and Protection.
> Nothing negative or harmful can get in,
> only positive good.

In essence, you are saying the protection is from God. You are protected from all negativity, but you do not want to close the door to positive things coming into your life.

This shield will protect you and it will also reflect the negativity back to whoever sent it threefold. You are not sending it. It is similar to a boomerang.

If you feel more comfortable, you can start the shield from below your feet and work up.

You can put it around yourself and around your bed before going to sleep. Put this White Light around whomever or whatever you wish.

Along the same lines, you can use four clear quartz crystals to protect your home. You only need the raw stones.

Place them at each point of the compass -- East, West, North and South.

If you are in an apartment, place one against each compass point next to the wall, not in each room. You can place them under a couch, in a planter, etc. They do not need to be visual, since you are utilizing their vibrations.

If you live in a house, place them as close to the foundation as possible. Bury them three-fourths of the way in the ground, so only one-fourth of the stone is above the surface. They will look like just ordinary stones to anyone seeing them.

Next do the Shield of Protection in a dome shape surrounding your home. Make sure the dome touches each stone. You can visualize the dome of White Light emanating from the stones also.

You never need to touch the stones again. However, you need to reinforce it by putting the Shield up every two or three months.

After you have been putting the Shield up for a time and feel comfortable with it, you will notice that it goes up very fast, perhaps after just the first few words.

When you get to this point, you need to choose a code word. Pick a word that represents the Shield to you, such as : Shield; Now; Up; Protection; Light, etc. -- whatever connects for you is fine.

Next, re-program your subconscious mind to know what the code word connects with. Before you put your Shield up, get in the habit of saying the code word first. When you feel comfortable with this, switch to just the code word -- the Shield will automatically go up.

There are also preventive measures you can put to use. Cancel fear and worry from your life. Entities can sense your fear and be attracted to it. That which you put energy into on a fear level will come to you. You will attract the conditions you fear. When you worry, distract the thought by thinking of the most positive things.

Practice positive thinking and action. Remember that thought creates your reality. As your level of Spirituality develops, your aura will become stronger and brighter. Your aura will deflect most negative attacks automatically.

Try to avoid people who are negative. They will drain you of your energy. We can't always stay away. Relatives are not always positive. But keep it to a minimum and put up your Shield.

All negative or positive vibrations automatically go back to their source when they are repelled by you, and you will no longer be a victim.

Anything you send out in thought comes back. If you wish someone harm, it rebounds to you threefold. Which would you rather have coming toward you? Easy answer, right?

If you feel like you are under attack, there are a few things you can do.

Always put up your Shield. When under attack, visualize the Shield three times a day minimum. Know it protects you and radiates the negativity back to the sender. You can also do other things in conjunction with your Shield. Sit with your legs crossed and cross your arms over you abdomen. This is a main target area as it is your solar plexus. Use prayers to counteract the negativity. Seek the help of Divine Power. You can also burn incense. Burn Frankincense or Sandalwood to change the vibration within your home. Burn with white or silver candles. Bless your home and place of work with Holy water or rose water. Do so in the name and through the power of Jesus Christ. You need to bless it in His name.

If you feel that you know who the person is that is attacking you, do not accept any gifts from him/her. They are sending negative vibrations. If you cannot turn a gift down without adding problems, then bless it immediately! You may have to deal with a relative or your boss. Try not to have the person in your home but if it is necessary, then try to make it on an infrequent basis.

If you received anything from the person in the past, preferably get rid of it. It is a psychic link connecting you to the person. This is one of the reasons cursed stones and rings work. Otherwise, Bless it.

Keep control over your hair, nail clippings, pictures of yourself and any other personal possession. Use caution in releasing information such as your birth date, what time you will be at a certain destination, etc.

If you have addictive tendencies, such as alcohol, keep out of bars or alcohol oriented situations (museums do not push alcohol). The psychic energies do not cease at these places. They build and attach to weak people.

When you are in a negative emotional relationship and you cannot seem to get out of it, visualize an umbilical cord of white light connecting you both from the solar plexus. Next visualize a giant knife or scissors of Love cutting the cord, releasing you both to your "Higher Good, to go in separate ways." After all, you do not wish the other person harm -- you merely want the person out of your life.

When a negative entity attacks you, send it Love, Bless it and send Healing Energy. If an entity attacks you, it has been sick. If you add your fear, anger or hatred, you are feeding it negative energy. This allows it to grow stronger and gives it power. It will double and then you will have it come back twice as hard to you. If you are sending the positive energy, basically you are canceling it out.

People are more open on a psychic level between 4:30 AM or PM and between 11:30 AM or PM to 12:00 AM or PM; therefore, these are the times to be especially cautious.

If a negative person is sending the attack and you think you know who the person is, Bless the person and surround him/her in White Light.

You are only sending positive. If you are wrong, have you ever known anyone who could not use an extra blessing? So you can never bless the wrong person.

Meditate because this will put you in a state of Higher Consciousness and thus negative energy will have a lesser effect on you.

You may wish to bless your home once a week. Prevention is also positive.

Do not accept guilt from anyone, or let them control you. Learn to say *"NO"* with conviction. Do not try to control others as that is also a form of negativity.

If you have to deal with negative people, do not stand or sit directly across from them, leaving yourself open to them. Avoid looking directly in their eyes. There is such a thing as the Evil Eye and negative energy can be focused from the eyes. Do not allow any face to face, direct level contact with them.

There are also baths which have been used for ages as a defense measure and for cleansing of energies. These baths change the vibration of the person by their properties. Water was used in the Bible for cleansing, and it has always signified the life force. It cleanses physically and mentally. When you take a bath for the purpose of a psychic result, it should be a separate time from your regular bath. Soap will also change the water's vibration. These Spiritual baths should always be used in conjunction with prayer and you should be immersed in the water. Stay in the water for ten to twenty minutes to receive the benefits. When you are finished, let yourself air dry. Do not use a towel on your body. You should not wash your hair for twenty-four hours after the bath.

SPIRITUAL BATH FORMULA

Make a tea from the herb or nut. Then add one cup to the bath water.

Some herbs (used separately) are:

Sage	Acacia	Burdock
Basil	Aloe	Ash
Cinnamon	Birch	Loosestrife
Nutmeg	Calamus	Yucca
St. John's Wort	Plantain	Heather
Dragon's Blood	Coconut	Ginseng

Valerian　　　　　　Devil's Shoestring　　　Mandrake

Or you can add 1/4 cup of baking soda to the water. Another bath can be with sea salt added. When you are through your bath clean the bathtub with vinegar to remove the negativity.

Other methods are gemstones, incense, candles, seals, flowers and numerous others. Remember, your strongest one is the Shield.

You need to cleanse your home after an argument so the energies do not collect and build up, causing stress at a later date.

Another method is to place approximately one teaspoon of sea salt in an eight ounce glass or bowl of water in each room of your home. Replace this each week. Throw the old water outside.

Have you ever noticed when you go to a friend's home, how you may feel immediately comfortable or uncomfortable? You are picking up the vibrations of the room, either positive or negative energies.

This book consists of numerous and varied formulas for attracting things into your life. You are working on a higher level and only want to tune into positive energy work full power. For this reason, psychic self-defense is imperative for your protection and the protection of those around you.

CHAPTER THREE

HERBAL MAGNETS

Occult Grimoire & Magical Formulary A Workbook For Creating A Positive Life

HERBAL MAGNETS

ATTRACTING YOUR NEEDS

Everything has its own vibration. Herbs work much the same as magnets in this respect. Whether you believe in the validity of the herbs to attract or not, they will still perform. Herbs have been utilized since ancient times for medicinal purposes as well as for protection and attraction.

Nature spirits are known and seen by some psychics and occultists. These spirits are very real and there are numerous varieties. They are representatives of the Divine Power and channels through which nature manifests. In working with these nature spirits we become aware of the properties of herbs and how to utilize them.

Think of these nature spirits as being of a broad range and type. Among these are spirits which look like tiny balls of white light, gnomes, and nature devas. They have intelligence and will. Some are similar to worker bees with a collective consciousness toward the same goal. These are all unseen forces cohabiting our world, with their own different levels. Some are the builders of plants. This is why when you talk to the plants or care for them, they grow better. You are really communicating with the spirit of the plant.

There have been times when my youngest son, Rob, has walked past a plant and said, "Excuse me." At times he sees white sparks of light flitting around the plant and does not want to disturb them. He is actually seeing the "building spirits" of the plant.

Children are very open to psychic input since they have not learned yet that they cannot "see".

There are various ways to attract your desires into your life, as well as into the lives of others. You will find some that are very powerful, while others simply do not work. The reason behind this is that some formulas have been, through ignorance, "modernized". In my work, I find the most powerful methods are the ancient ones. They may sound simple at times, or not as mysterious as you would like. However, the simple methods are not diluted and added onto for dramatics; hence they are strong. The newer ones have many ingredients that are not necessary. This is to impress others. If you look at a formula that calls for fifteen ingredients, some of which are very difficult to find, you will be very impressed by the person who writes it. If you knew that only three were needed, it would not seem as impressive. By adding the unneeded things, they are actually taking away the strength.

I always feel that in working with nature, use the simpler and stronger ways. Then you will always get positive results and full strength.

The basics for Spiritual work should be known. It is important to know what results to expect.

LOVE

This covers a vast territory. Positive emotions, communication, sexual fulfillment, partnership, warmth, sharing. Every person may have their own concept of love. When working with magic, it should be positive in order to attract the right person into your life. Don't try to coerce someone to love you. The vibrations will attract new friends, new relationships. They will put you in a situation where you will meet more people. You will communicate better, send off more feelings of warmth for others to pick up. You will attract a new partner. Once you bring the person into your life, it is up to you to keep the relationship going.

MONEY

This may come in as more cash flow, or as the possession you wanted. It may also put you in situations for more money opportunities to come in, such as a promotion, new job, more financial sense in business decisions, or someone repaying a loan.

LUCK

The vibrations of any luck formula you use will put you in the right place, at the right time. It can come in many forms. Used mainly when you need to turn your luck around.

COURT

People you deal with will be more receptive to your side, less easily angered.

JOB

Being at the correct place when opportunity opens a door, communicating more easily in an interview. Others becoming more aware of your abilities.

The following formulae should be used to help others as well as yourself. Start to improve your life now. The herbs are meant to be used on a vibratory level and not to be taken internally.

Use the formulae with Power, Truth and Love.

May God Bless you in His Work.

LOVE SPELLS

COUCH GRASS

Sprinkle some of the grass under your mattress to attract a new lover. Works in a short time.

DEVIL'S SHOE STRING

To bring back a lover, take some dirt from his left footprint along his path. Add some Devil's Shoe String and place this in one of his socks or her stocking. Then place it into your closet.

MANDRAKE ROOT

Carry this root with you at all times to attract love into your life.

ADAM AND EVE ROOT

Used in a pair. To hold a relationship together, carry one each.

To attract, a woman would give a man an Adam root. A man would give an Eve root to a woman.

LOVE CHARM

In a red pouch, carry a little of each herb mixed together.

Lavender	Rose Buds
Two Tonka Beans	Vervain
Vanilla Bean	Couch Grass

Concentrate on what you want as you mix these. Then add a little Attraction Powder.

VERVAIN

Carried in a red pouch will attract love and bring luck to the one wearing it.

PASSION

1/2 oz. Orris Root powder	1/2 oz. Lavender
1/2 oz. Anise Seed	4 oz. Rose powder
1/4 oz. Saltpeter	1/2 oz. Red Clover

Use this as an herbal incense. Burn self-igniting charcoal until it is burning strongly, then sprinkle the blend over it. Concentrate on your desire. On a piece of white paper using red ink, write the name of the person five times. Then use a match to light it and burn it to ashes in a dish or over the incense. When you have done this, throw it outside to the wind. Do this for seven days. Use two or three drops of Love Oil each morning to achieve the results.

DRUNKEN COCONUT

Offered to Eleggua to ask for his help in gaining the love of the person you want. Cut off the top of a coconut and empty it. Fill with caramels, gumdrops and five types of liquor. Add the essences: Essencia de Menta, de Amor, Dominante, Vencedora and Sigueme.

A cigar is lit in the name of Eleggua and smoke blown through the shell. The top is put back quickly to keep in the smoke, then sealed together with a candle that was bought in a church. The coconut stands for the head of the person you want. A white candle is lit in the name of Eleggua for five consecutive days, asking for the love of the person you want.

TO BREAK A LOVE SPELL

LILY

Carry a fresh lily if you think someone used a love spell on you. This will break it. The lotus seeds can also be used for this purpose.

TO ATTRACT NEW FRIENDS

LOVE SEED

Known to be used by the American Indians. They carry the seed of the herb called Love Seed.

LUCKY HAND

Soak the herb overnight in Rose Oil. The next day, start wearing it over your heart. This herb has the distinct shape of a hand.

MANDRAKE ROOT

Take a Mandrake Root and carve the name of the person you want into the root. As you do this, tell it what you want to be done.

Add Red Clover, Rose and a piece of Willow. Wrap all the ingredients in a piece of red satin and place this under your bed.

MONEY ATTRACTIONS

LEMON

Hang a whole uncut lemon up in your home. You can use a string, wire or anything else convenient. Money starts coming in within seven days. Personally, I hang it in my kitchen. When anyone asks about it, I say it is a room freshener. This prevents any negative energy from being sent by a person who does not understand.

FENUGREEK

Carry this herb in a green pouch to attract finance.

ORRIS ROOT

Can be carried in a green pouch or in your pocket, pocketbook or wallet.

GAMBLING

Make a tea from the flowers of the chamomile plant. Gamblers wash their hands in it before playing cards for good luck.

Or carry Jamaica Ginger or carry Five Finger Root.

WEALTH

Carry Red Clover in a red pouch, and carry it with you.

Ingredients for a Mojo Bag: Mix equal parts of each herb.

Alfalfa	Basil
Mandrake	Grains of Paradise
Jasmine	Sesame
Golden Seal	

MONEY DRAWING BAG

Use a green pouch. Add the following mixed:

1 Orris Root	2 Tonka Beans
Nutmeg	Alfalfa
Sage	Chamomile
2 or 3 Cloves	

Also add a Jade gemstone and sprinkle Money Drawing Powder over the blend.

BRINGING IN MONEY ON A POWER LEVEL

Cut a small hole in the top of a nutmeg. Hollow this out. Place mercury into the hole. Next, melt a green candle over it until it covers the hole to seal it. When you are done, carry it with you.

DEVIL'S SHOESTRING ROOT

For money or to help in court cases, carry this herb wrapped in parchment paper. On the paper, in Dove's Blood ink or red ink, write what you need done.

BLACK SNAKE ROOT

When carried in a green bag, will pull money in for you.

LAVENDER OR LOW JOHN THE CONQUEROR

To attract luck with finance, place this herb in a green pouch. Add a penny, a nickel, a quarter and a dollar bill. Carry this and the money will multiply seven times.

NUTMEG

Use a piece of parchment paper. Write in Dove's Blood ink or red ink the amount of money you want to come to you. Wrap the parchment around a whole nutmeg and carry it with your change.

TONKA BEANS

Carry two in a green Conjure Bag. Moisten them with two or three drops of Money Drawing Oil.

TO FIND MONEY

Place the following in a green Mojo Bag:

    Smartweed   Lodestone   Gold Magnetic Sand

TO DRAW MONEY

In a red pouch, place a green Lodestone. Then place a Patchouli herb over it. Anoint the bag with Money Drawing Oil. Place the bag in a dark place where others will not touch it, for seven days. After the seven days, take it out and start to carry it with you. Money will be drawn to you.

NEST EGGS

Make a nest out of the herbs Khuss Khuss about three inches round. Put one seed of Buckeye or Orris Root in the middle. Wrap money around it, and put into a safe place (deposit box, safe, etc.).

When you get money, put a percentage of it away with your nest egg everyday. It will multiply. Give it a name to personalize it. Don't tell anyone about it. Then ask yourself if you've tried to follow in God's path today and if you have remembered to thank Him for what you already have.

Say:

Lord, as I place my daily savings with my nest egg,
may I be thankful for your blessings.
May I see the money and prosperity multiply
as I seek Your path of light.
For it comes from the Universal supply and by Divine
Right, under Grace and in a Perfect way.
Life's prosperity is mine, and I know God
will take care of me.
Amen

ATTRACT RICHES INTO YOUR HOME

Boil Fenugreek seeds as an infusion. Scrub the floors with it in every room in your house. Place a few seeds along with small pieces of Orris Root in each room and leave them there. Change the seeds and root once a week.

COURT

TO WIN A CASE

Carry marigold in your pocket when you are in court. The morning that you go to court, add marigolds to your bath water to be thought of favorably.

FOR COURT

Cut a lemon in half. Put salt on one half and wrap it in a new linen handkerchief. Do the same with the other half. Put one in your pocket or purse. Before going into the courtroom, rub one of the lemon halves briskly on your hands, towards you. When you enter the court, take the other half and squirt the juice into your hand. Read Psalm #23; this will help win your case.

TO CARRY INTO COURT

Buckthorn; Marigold; or Sacred Bark. You can carry these herbs individually or place them in a white pouch.

INFUSION

Make an infusion of Sacred Bark. Sprinkle it around your home before going to court. This will help you win.

PROTECTION

ACACIA

It is placed over the bed or doorway to keep away evil.

CACTUS

If kept in your home, it is said to keep burglars away. Draws negative energy to it so the energy does not come to you. If kept outside, it is good protection. Place one at each point of the compass.

MYRTLE

Keep this herb in the corners of your kitchen to protect yourself from hunger and lack of money to buy food.

PROTECTION FROM ILLNESS

To have less frequent health problems, and to speed up your natural healing process, carry two Tonka Beans in a green pouch around your neck.

BATHS FOR PROTECTION AND CLEANSING

Baths change your vibrations by their properties. Down through the ages water has been the symbol of life. It cleanses us physically and mentally. Have you ever noticed how relaxed and good you feel while soaking in a tub?

When you use a bath for protection, do not use this time to cleanse the physical self. Use full immersion and prayer. Do not use soap. Soak for ten to twenty minutes.

Nut baths and herbal baths are used the same way. Make a tea from the herbs. Use one cup in your tub water. Some herbs which are used for this purpose are:

Rose	Olive	Fennel	Clove
Wormwood	Mandrake	Hazel	Birch
Basil	Cinnamon	Nutmeg	Coffee
Sage	Acacia	Mugwort	Burdock
Aloe	Anise	Horehound	Yucca
St. John Wort	Sandalwood	Holly	Linden
Vervain	Parsley	To	Valerian

When you're finished, use ammonia to clean the tub. This will life the negative vibrations from the tub.

TO PROTECT YOUR FAMILY

Have them carry some of these herbs:

Heather
Grass
Carnation
Peony
Mistletoe
Wahoo Bark
Bloodroot
Violet
Devil's Shoestring

Thyme
Loosestrife
Ginseng

HOME PROTECTION

Add *Beth Root* to incense used for protection. Sprinkle around the room of your home. Pick the roots when the moon is waning and dry them. When dry, cut them into small pieces and string them on a white or red thread. Wear them as a necklace.

PROTECTION FROM NEGATIVE SPIRITS

Sprinkle *Solomon's Seal Root* in the corners of every room of your home. Anoint the windows and doors with *Protection Oil* by running your fingers along the frames on the inside of your home. Do this in the name of The Father, Son and Holy Spirit. Burn *Protection Incense* or *Tobacco Incense*.

PROTECTION FROM CURSES

Carry two of the *Gilead* buds to protect yourself from hexes, curses and the evil eye.

PROTECTION OF YOUR HOUSE WHILE YOU ARE AWAY

Blend the following ingredients in this formula as incense. Burn it the night before you leave and on the morning of your departure.

4 oz. Myrrh	4 oz. Sandalwood powder
2 oz. Lavender	2 oz. Winter bark
4 oz. Coconut powder	3 oz. Vetivert
3 oz. Cypress	1 oz. Saltpeter

Place ingredients which are not in powder form in a mortar. Grind them down as much as you can with a pestle. Add the powders. Gives off a very powerful vibration for protection.

One of my clients used this protection before he went on a vacation to the Bahamas. Robert knew he was safe and nothing would be taken from his home so he enjoyed the trip and came home in a very happy mood. His house was just as he left it.

The next day he saw one of the neighbors who told him that the house next door had been robbed, though nobody was away on a trip. These neighbors couldn't understand why that house was robbed when the one next to it was empty and had easier entry.

Of course, we know why. When you work with Spiritual Laws, nothing can go wrong.

GET RID OF EVIL - TO BE SAFE

Put an egg into a new glass. Fill the glass with water. Invoke Saint Claire to bring peace and harmony into your life. Light a white candle in her honor. Repeat this for nine days. At the end of this time throw the water into the street. Take the egg to a park and smash it to the ground. Invoke Saint Claire to ask that as the egg was broken, so will evil go out of your life.

TO CHANGE VIBRATIONS

Let a *Garlic* bulb soak in a glass of water for an hour, then wet your fingers with the garlic water and tap the windows in your home. This will keep negative spirits out. It does not bother positive spirits. Keep a garlic clove above your doorway to keep negativity out.

PROPHETIC DREAMS

During dreams, you tune into information numerous times, much of which is prophecy. You may want to be more aware of the information. The following formulae show you how to bring these dreams in.

FIVE FINGER GRASS

The five points of the leaves attract love, money, power, health and wisdom. Some of the wisdom is shown to you in your dreams.

Place a few of the fresh cut leaves under your pillow to attract prophetic dreams and to sleep restfully.

BRACKEN

Place the Bracken root under your pillow. Concentrate on your problems as the last thought before you sleep. You will have a dream which gives you the solution.

JASMINE

Burn this herb with Jasmine incense before sleep. This will cause prophetic dreams.

One of my clients decided to use this method. Maurice was keeping track of the information each morning on a pad. He noticed in three dreams, all during the same night, he had the same combination of numbers come up in various forms. He saw a basket of fruit and noticed how strange it was that it only contained one apple, four oranges and nine peaches.

He ignored this. Next, he saw dice with the same order of numbers -- one, four, nine. Still he ignored this, since he did not use numbers for any purpose normally.

Once again it came up as he watched a cruise ship pulling out of the harbor. He dreamt he was walking to his cabin door, numbered one-four-nine.

Maurice decided he could definitely take a "hint". The next day he played those numbers for the week. In two days it hit.

Your dreams may not always come in as his did, but you need to keep track. Pay more attention to them. You never know how informative the dream will be.

MUGWORT

Placed under your pillow, it will increase prophetic dreams. If it is placed near the bed, it aids in astral projection. Near to you, it will protect you.

Herbs are an ancient force which we can use to our benefit. They were utilized by Merlin and Moses, by the Egyptians, Hungarians, Norsemen, Africans, Swedes, and all other cultures. To have survived all this time and through all these varied cultures tells us that there must be metaphysical truth behind it.

CHAPTER FOUR

TREASURE MAPPING

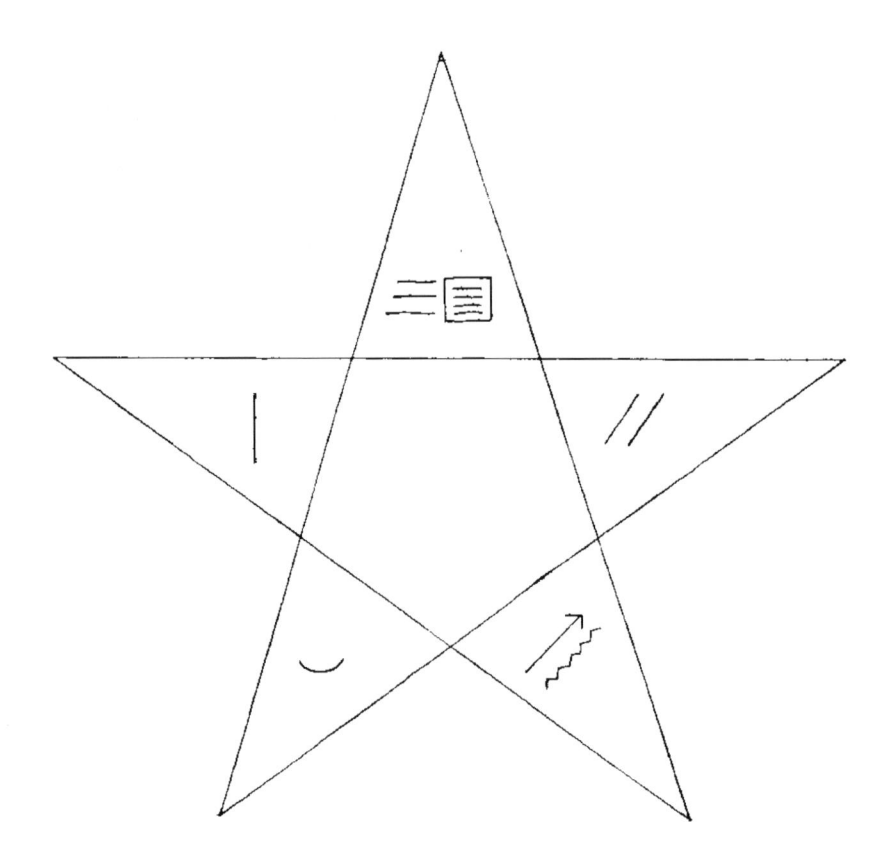

Occult Grimoire & Magical Formulary A Workbook For Creating A Positive Life

TREASURE MAPPING

Treasure mapping is a form of visualization. It is the outward visualizing of the inward process of choosing a definite goal; then consciously working towards a result.

There are various types of treasure maps. The purpose varies -- health, love, money, job, prosperity, a new home, success -- the list can go on endlessly. Someone once said, "If you can think of it, you can map for it". This is very true in a literal sense.

There are two main types:

1. This is a map nobody else will ever see. You may be as open as you would like in what you put into it.

2. There is a possibility or a definite chance another person will see it and you do not want them to know what you are doing. In this case, you would use a code (such as when you are still living at home or with family).

Some people keep their treasure map out in full view, while others prefer privacy. You can make them in the lid of a shoe box, in your notebook, in a drawer, or even make it small enough to fit into your wallet.

This method has also been called "pictured prayer". It keeps us focused on our goals and reinforces that God wants us to have all of our needs met now, not maybe at some distant date.

The Bible tells us that there is a power in the word. When we think or verbalize, we are in essence creating our own reality. We are putting physical form to our world.

The treasure map also keeps us focused on our beliefs -- on God and the Christ Light. It makes us realize that everything in our lives manifests through Him. It reminds us of our connection, our Oneness with God. We are utilizing the treasure map to aid us in having God work with and through us.

We are co-creators of our world. We deserve to have our needs and wants met.

The map will help you to keep your life in motion towards your goals. To know that what you desire is now coming in through the Father. Remember, "Ask and is shall be given you". He will not let you fail. Sometimes it can come in faster than at other times. However, the outcome will be success.

You can use the treasure map to bring in anything. You can also use it to help change a negative thought pattern, a habit, to help others, or to become more spiritual.

We need to work on two levels:

1. Treasure Mapping - Metaphysical reality
2. Going by Guidance - Physical reality

As an example:

    I taught Jim, a friend of mine, how to treasure map to bring in a better job. Jim did everything that needed to be done on a metaphysical level. However, he never looked in the newspaper or went out of his way to find this better position. One day he called and told me he did not understand why for the last three days he had had a strong urge to call a friend with whom he had lost contact a long time ago. I suggested that he follow the guidance and make the phone call.

    Jim made the call that same day and they rekindled the friendship. During their reunion, the subject of looking for a better job came up. It turned out that the friend knew of a job vacancy which sounded perfect. The contacts were made and Jim got the job.

    Jim almost missed this opportunity because he failed to make the effort of contacting friends, checking the newspaper, etc.

    Treasure mapping is meant to pull in results; however, you need to work on both realities. If you have an urge or hunch, follow it. This may be the way you are being shown to move.

    This is a fun way to keep you in motion towards your prosperity and to keep the God awareness constant.

    The more we focus on our goals, the faster they will be met.

CREATING YOUR MAP

Make it as simple as possible. Larger ones may be seen easier at more of a distance. Smaller ones may be more private and easily carried.

You need a piece of paper to paste or draw on. Oakboard is also good. You will need to make vivid pictures, preferably in color. Color aids in focusing your attention. Also, we retain colors more easily.

Choose what you want as your goal. You will be working definitely towards it. Make it something you want, not what others think you need. Start with the one most important to you.

My older son, Rick, years ago wanted a ten-speed bicycle. He focused on it and worked with it. He "knew" he was getting it for Christmas. It was definite and Rick started to plan where he would go with it and how he would take care of it. At that time it was not financially possible. But he was sure and focused on it faithfully.

A few weeks before Christmas, business picked up above the usual level. Then an excellent sale came up. Everything seemed to fall into place and we could afford to give him that bicycle. So, even though it did not seem logically possible when he started working on it, he received his bicycle for Christmas.

You can choose a color for the background paper on which to glue your pictures:

Pink -	for health
Deep Pink or Red -	for love
Grass Green or Gold -	for Prosperity
Orange -	for Energy
Sky Blue or Clear Yellow -	for Spiritual Development
Lavender -	for Service

Maps need words or written affirmations. There is power in the written thought or spoken word.

The Bible tells us we can have what we want. In the center of your map, always use a picture of the Christ, or another God symbol - a Bible, a Cross, Church, or whatever signifies to you that God is the One Source of All There Is.

It is extremely important not to forget to add money or finances of some sort to your map, if the desired outcome needs financing.

A check made out to you, paid in full, and signed by the Universal Bank is good. You can also use play money. If you see a picture of money in a magazine, it can also be used on your map.

We use maps in our lives to find our way on roads, to museums, to numerous places we need to go. This map leads you to your needs and highest good.

Each day you need to use your map for visualization. You can do this fifteen or twenty minutes at a time, or look at your map continuously on and off all day to give you focus.

Always give thanks to God for this or something better, and for the good of all concerned. This sets up an attitude of expectancy.

Next, release your thoughts of what is on your map. Go and do something else. As you do so, you are planting your seeds of faith in the "Universal Garden".

Do the visualization every day to "water the seeds that you have planted" and watch them grow.

It is very important to let only those who are involved with your treasure mapping to be told about it. Do not tell anyone who is not supportive of what you are doing. You may have negative feedback from people who are of a doubtful or arrogant temperament. This can delay your results from manifesting. You may also subconsciously accept some of their doubts. "When you mix your White thoughts with their Black thoughts, you are going to get Gray thoughts". This brings confusion to what you are mapping for and a divergence of your focus.

It is of more benefit to you to keep the treasure mapping a secret. Remember that when you work with the laws of manifestation, you need to do everything that you can to bring the creation in. When you do your part and act on your hunches, the ideas given to you by Divine Guidance, your ideas will begin to come to pass. Unexpected doors will open even with desires you were not conscious of yet.

You can also place more than one desire on a map. Use one at first until you get the feel of it. Later, when you add more, section it off with a line.

Another method is the Pentagram. This can be used only for material needs such as cars, food, house, money, etc., and should be used mainly with code. This is effective if you know others may run across your map, or if you want to use a poster board on your wall without anyone understanding what you are working on.

ALWAYS make sure the five pointed star has the single point at the top, and the two at the bottom. Picture a man with two feet on the ground, arms outstretched, head erect. This is positive. When you see it reversed, it is being used for negative purposes. We only work on a positive plane.

You need to answer five questions about what you want to bring in - *What, Where, Why, When, How*. Place one answer within each point of the star.

To make the code, think of what you can put on paper that others will not understand, yet when you look at it, you will know what it represents. When working with the Pentagram, always use a white background and black ink. White represents positive and Divine Power. Black represents power.

EXAMPLE:

WHAT -   What represents a car to you? Part of a wheel, legal paper (Ownership - you could draw a rectangle), or the speed lines behind a car such as drawn on cartoons?

WHERE - Where do you want the car? You want it in your driveway, so you could draw two parallel lines to represent this.

WHY -   To go to work, or to better your life, or whatever reason. To better your life, you could draw an arrow pointing up, or a stairway (you are climbing upward).

WHEN -   Now. Everything is now, immediately. If you indicate a later time, it will always be later. You can draw a smile (you are happy that it manifested), or the rays of the sun (for happiness).

HOW -   Through Divine Power - God. You can draw one line of the cross. You will know what it means.

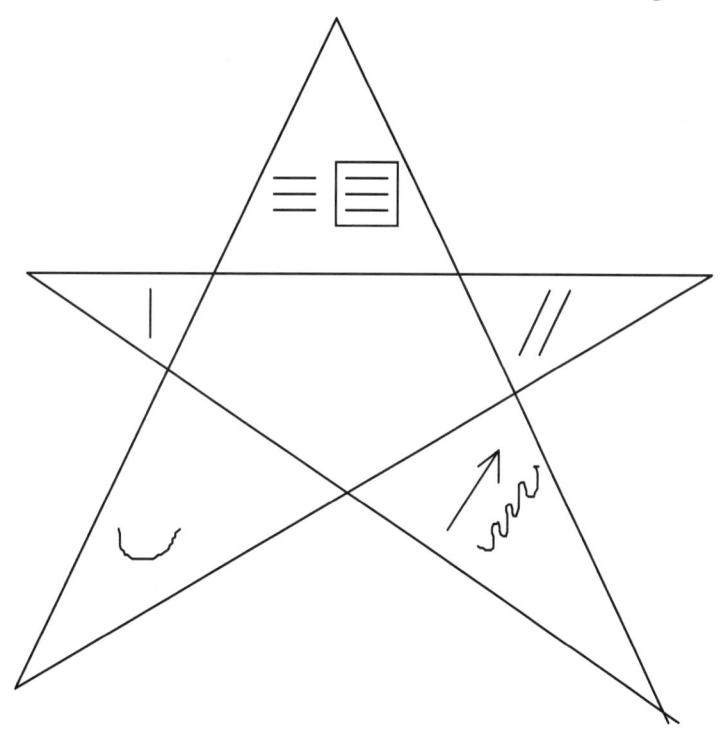

Then, every day you look at it and read each star point. It is similar to reading a story.

Always thank God for His work. When you put this technique into motion, consider it done. So thank God for it.

<u>AFFIRMATIONS</u>

This will give you an idea of some positive thoughts and written affirmations to put on your treasure map.

Through Divine Power. This is important. Everything we manifest comes from God. We need to acknowledge this.

In A Perfect Way. This needs to be on all maps. You want things in a positive way, not because others are not doing well.

This or Better. You do not want to close a door. You may want an older car due to lack of finance. You could receive a newer one because someone lowered a price to move it faster, or bought a new one for themselves and gave you theirs. Whatever way, do not close the door to better.

Nothing is too much to ask God. God said He wanted us to do well. Not in one or two areas, but in all things.

God is the source of all my good. Used as an acknowledgment.

"Peace Be Within Thy Walls, And Prosperity Within Thy Palaces". This is good on a map for a new home.

I Give Thanks For My New ... Whatever you are mapping for - car, house, perfect relationship, health, etc.

I am always loved. For relationship, friendships.

My perfect partner shall come to me. For relationships, friendships.

I live in the law of abundance and God is in charge of my Bank Account. For business, finances.

I am well and happy. For health.

I am healed and strong. For health.

Thank you, Father, for my better job. If you have a specific place, add that in.

I always get along in peace and joy with my landlord. Co-workers, boss, aunt, etc.

God shows me what to do. Then also listen to your intuition.

God knows what is best for me. To handle situations, etc.

I am loved by all and I love all people. You attract what you send out.

I prosper more every day. Work towards finance or emotional prosperity.

I reach my goals. Keeps you focused.

I am happy and live in the love of God. For peace and happiness.

I am reaching my success. Whatever area success is to you.

I am ... A lawyer (working towards this goal), happily married, healthy, contented, spiritual, etc.

The Lord God takes care of me, He provides for me. Acknowledging your belief that God will take care of all your needs.

Make your own affirmations. Put them in positive ways only.

Eve wanted a better home for herself and her family. She loved her friend's house and decided to treasure map for one just like it. She drew a cross in the middle of a gold poster board, then drew a circle around it. Next, she found a colored picture of a house similar to the type she wanted and pasted it on. She pasted pictures of a bright kitchen, a happy family. She added a picture of dollar signs (from a car ad) because once she moved in, she needed to be able to afford it financially. She didn't want to manifest the house, only to lose it. She even pasted in a flower bed.

Eve wrote the following affirmation on the map in various places:

> Through Divine Power
> In a Perfect Way
> This or Something Better.
> Thank You, Father, for my new beautiful,
> peaceful, happy home.
> For the good of all concerned,
> God supplies my every need.

Eve knew it was coming in. She would look at her map every day, feeling happy and knowing it would manifest at its own perfect pace.

Eight months later, her friend told her she was moving to another state. Her husband had a better job offer with a much higher salary and they decided to take it.

She said they knew how much Eve loved their house, and if she wanted to buy it, they would lower their price. They would rather sell to someone who appreciated it and would take good care of it.

Eve and her husband bought the house and everyone was happy.

Since Eve put on the map "In A Perfect Way", she not only received the same type of house she loved, but the actual house she loved. It was also perfect because her friends moved due to accepting a better job, not because they became insolvent and were forced to sell their home at a low price. It was good for everyone, and they all remained close friends.

When you treasure map, do so with joy and happiness. You will receive what you desire and that should make you feel joy. God is manifesting something good into your life for you. How can you not feel joy when you are feeling the Unity of God?

If your earthly father takes care of you, how much more so will your Heavenly Father take care of you? He has already promised to supply whatever you ask for.

So do this with fun, joy and thanks. Know as you ask, you have already been answered.

CHAPTER FIVE

RITUAL OILS

RITUAL OILS

Oils were used by the Magi, as well as by many other of the ancients and adepts of the times, when communicating with their Higher Selves.

Chaldean Priests, mystics, adepts, psychics, and religious orders of all types, to name a few, utilize the magnetic force of the oils. Many people are sensitive to the aroma, color and vibrational influence of oils.

During the time of the Renaissance, talismans, gems of power on goblets, and use of the occult were widely spread. It is no wonder that perfumes and oils were rampant. Oils were used to attract love and to keep it. It was as well used to heighten lust, in which case it was only on a physical level, not emotional.

Oils were also used for protection or whatever was needed at the time. Sorcerers claimed to utilize the oils for commanding others in conjunction with Divine Will. This made them very popular in those times of feuding and power struggles.

You can place two or three drops of the oil you choose on the palm of your hand. Mystics do this before shaking hands with the person on whom they are working. As they shake hands or make some form of contact by touch, they look into the eyes of the person, and concentrate on what they want from that person.

You can wear the oil and be within three feet of the person to have it work on an aromatic level or on a magnetic attraction level.

You can use the oil to anoint candles and so dress them. Altars may be anointed once a week. Mojo bags may be anointed every week.

Put oils into baths, then concentrate on your desires.

To cleanse and protect your home, add oils to the floor washing water.

Another ancient method used by mystics is to anoint your palms with the oil. Next, anoint a candle, forming a circle around it. Consecrate the oil before use with a prayer or repeating a Psalm.

The following methods are meant to aid in gaining your needs and wants in a positive form, not to control. Decide on your needs prior to starting.

FOR MAGICAL WORK

The Mystics and Magi utilized this method to call in Spirit for aid.

Mixture is a blend of: Myrrh
Galingale
Cinnamon
Pure olive oil

MAGNETIC OIL

You can magnetize any oil which you feel you need to strengthen in order to help you draw in.

Place the oil over a lodestone or magnet. Repeat a Psalm or a prayer of your choice. Leave it overnight during a full moon before using it.

LOVE ATTRACTION

Use two or three drops of the Love Oil on the palm of your hand every morning. Concentrate on the person you desire; otherwise you will get many different kinds of people (fall out!). That is all right if you do not have a special person in mind, but you should then concentrate on some of the qualities you would like. For example: warm, tall, etc.

LOVE OILS

Love Oil is the best oil to use for love; however, if it is not available, you may use Success Oil instead.

Do not use any form of oil that is negative since you do not want to control. After all, you can get better results by working in a positive way.

MAGNETIC OIL FOR PSYCHIC POWERS

Blend together:　　Cassia　　　　Sandalwood
　　　　　　　　　Lilac　　　　　Tuberose
　　　　　　　　　Mimosa　　　　Acacia
　　　　　　　　　Nutmeg

SUCCESS

Use Ylang Ylang each morning and each night. Concentrate on what you want as success.

HEX-BREAKING

Blend together:　　Myrrh
　　　　　　　　　Dandelion
　　　　　　　　　Rosemary
　　　　　　　　　Cloves

HAPPINESS

Blend: Sweet Pea

Apple Blossom

Wear two or three drops of the blend every morning. Go out knowing that things are coming to you. They do.

LUCKY LIFE

Blend: Cypress

Lotus

Place a few drops on the palm of your hands. Rub them together and concentrate on luck coming into your life.

Remember to say, "Thank you Lord," for it is already there as you ask.

LOVE

Blend: Jasmine

Rose

Clove

Wear the blend on attract your desires. Focus on who, or what type of person you want when you put this on.

LOVE ATTRACTION

Blend: Gardenia
         Jasmine
         Plumeria

Use four or five drops in your bathtub water. Soak fifteen or twenty minutes, concentrating on your desire.

Do not use soap when you bathe at this time. This is used as a Spiritual Bath.

MAGNETIC OIL TO ATTRACT MEN

Blend: Lavender   Ambergris
         Musk   Tonka
         Jasmine   Ginger

Use only a few drops. For women ONLY to wear. Very Powerful blend.

MAGNETIC OIL TO ATTRACT WOMEN

Blend: Patchouli   Civet

Occult Grimoire & Magical Formulary A Workbook For Creating A Positive Life

Violet	Bay
Musk	Vetivert

Wear ONLY if you are male. Powerful tool to attract women. Once attracted, you keep it going on your own.

ENERGY

Blend: Allspice
          Vanilla
          Rosemary

Heightens your vitality level at the time you have it on.

PSYCHIC ABILITY

Blend:	Lotus	Cassia
	Lilac	Sandalwood
	Mimosa	

Heightens you awareness. Try wearing this during meditation.

HOUSE CLEANING

In a pail of water, add: Clove   Olive
                           Myrrh   Sandalwood

Next, wash all your floors with this blend. Negativity will not be able to stay in the room.

STUDY

Blend or use separately: Honeysuckle
                           Lilac

Heightens your mental powers which will enable you to study more effectively.

ATTRACT FRIENDS

Wear Sweet Pea to bring in new friends. It is up to you after they come in, to keep it going.

MONEY

Blend: Pine

Vervain

Place a few drops (two or three) on your wallet each day and visualize money bulging from it.

State: My mind and thoughts control reality.

SLEEP

Place a few drops of Lavender Oil on a cloth to be placed under your pillow or directly on your pillow.

You may also choose to make an herbal bag containing Lavender and anoint it with Lavender Oil. Next, place the herbal bag under your pillow. The aroma will help induce calm, natural, peaceful sleep.

POWER

Blend: Carnation
          Vanilla

When worn, this will heighten your natural power. Make sure to use it on a positive level.

All people have intentions, and what those are can come to pass. So stay Positive. Use Power discreetly.

FAST MONEY

Put two drops of Money Oil on an Orris Root. Concentrate on money coming in NOW. Carry it with you in your pocket or pocketbook at all times.

Bless the Orris Root in the name of God.

NEW HOME

Blend: High John
Holy Oil
Success Oil Mixture
Money Oil Mixture

Dress a green Seven Day Candle with this oil blend.

After a bath or shower previous to going out, put a few drops on the bottom of both feet and into the palms of your hand, and over your Third Eye (middle of your forehead).

Pray Psalm #61 until you obtain your new home.

Visualize the type of house you want every day until your house comes in.

Rev. Maurice Ramsey also used this method. He had a client come to him as a last resort. The family wanted the house of their dreams. They had a picture of the particular house they had wanted for the last fifteen years.

Rev. Ramsey told them to use this formula and place the picture of the house on an altar setting. The altar consisted of a white cloth in an area where it wouldn't be disturbed. The green Seven Day candle was placed in the middle. The picture of the house was placed on the right side of the candle, the oil blend on the left side. Lastly, they placed the Bible, opened to Psalm #61, directly in front of the candle, to see the house, feel it was theirs. They did this every day.

As they started to use this formula, the money for the down payment started to come in.

The family bought the home of their dreams in a few months later.

The means for obtaining your home may come in several forms. One of the main ways this will occur is through your dream state. You will start seeing numbers. They are meant to be utilized to play -- whatever you play that uses the numbers. It is one of the ways to build your cash flow.

PEACE AT WORK

Blend:	Gardenia
Tuberose
Cumin

Prior to leaving for work, put a few drops in the palm of your hand and on your Third Eye. Concentrate on being calm and serene.

When you are at work, bless everyone and send Peace and Love to them. If they upset you, be calm and bless them again.

After all, you cannot be too upset with people who do not know any better. They are still working from a level of unawareness.

MENTAL POWER

Blend:
- Honeysuckle
- Lilac
- Cassia

Place some drops on dried Lilac herbs. Put it in a Simmer Pot and light it. Use in the same room where you study or work.

MONEY MAGNET

Blend together:
- Almond
- Bayberry
- Yellow Root
- Vervain
- Pine

Place two or three drops on your fingers. Rub the oil around the edge of your wallet starting at the top left corner. Do not break contact as you go clockwise until you get back to where you started.

Next, place two or three drops in the palm of your hands and rub them together.

Money automatically comes to you, as well as opportunities for even greater monetary flow.

My friend, Robert, was a skeptic at first about the use of oils; however, due to some minor financial problems, he asked if he could try a bottle of the Money Oil.

That particular week my mother was taking my son, Rob, and me to San Diego on vacation. Robert agreed to check up on our house and care for our parrot while we were gone.

The third day I was away, Robert tried the Money Oil for the very first time. On his way home from my house he turned the corner to his apartment and right next to the phone booth he usually called me from he spotted a fifty dollar bill.

The day before I came home, as he was returning from checking up on our house, he found a twenty dollar bill.

The day I arrived home, Robert stopped by, amazed at what had happened. On his way home this time, he found a billfold with seventy dollars in it.

It doesn't always work in the same manner, but money does come in.

MEDICINE BAG FOR LOVE ATTRACTION

Use a red bag. Add a mixture of:

    1/4 tsp. Couch Grass

    1/4 tsp. Linden Flowers

    7 Rose Buds

    2 Tonka Beans

    1/4 tsp. Vervain

    1/4 tsp. Lavender

    1/8 tsp. Attraction Power

Tie the bag closed with three knots.

Place two or three drops of Love oil in the palm of your hands and rub the bag between them.

Concentrate on the name of the person you want. Visualize how you want the person (marriage, date, etc.). Remember to say: *In A Perfect Way.*

Carry this medicine bag with you at all times until the results you want come in.

A NOTE ON CUTTING THE OILS

When you use the oils, you can proceed with the following method for cutting the blends or for one pure oil.

Cutting it means you are not utilizing it full force or pure. You are diluting it.

Many stores will sell them cut, since it is less expensive or it may be that the aroma is too intense when pure.

When you mix, use 40% oil and 60% of whichever ingredient you choose to cut it with.

For cutting, use any one of the following: Glycerin, Alcohol, Cutting Oil, Olive Oil.

I never cut the oils since I want them full force. However, it is your option.

Remember, you want the full power to work for you. Experiment and see which way you prefer.

CHAPTER SIX

CANDLE MAGIC

Occult Grimoire & Magical Formulary A Workbook For Creating A Positive Life

CANDLE MAGIC

RECEIVE YOUR BURNING DESIRES

Candle magic is an ancient art which has prevailed down through the centuries, still in dominant use today. Even though it is not called candle magic, candles are burned in churches for loved ones who have passed away; for healing of an ill person. They are also used in altar settings today much as they were of old. The Bible mentions light in many forms.

Fire worship was known in many cultures. Though not always understood, it was acknowledged as a Power Force. Sun Worship included the fire element.

The main religions of our time all use the candle as a positive force.

The candle is also a cleansing force. It purifies and protects against negativity.

Fire was regarded as sacred. It was considered the Life Force -- providing warmth for survival against the cold of winter, means for cooking, as well as protection from wild animals. The uses are too numerous to be detailed here.

Ritual magic, as all magic, knows how to put this force to work for us.

We use candles as a simple and powerful tool. It does not need to be complicated. Mainly it acts as a focus for your petition to Divine Power. You only need to focus on your request, visualize it as done, use your inner will and you will bring it in. Your mental thought puts it into motion and your will keeps it moving in the correct direction until the work is completed.

Candles can be used for many negative intentions. However, since I only work on a positive level, all the formulas are positive. (I like my Karma.) Candles are always used in conjunction with prayers or affirmations. This is an awareness of where your Power comes from to do this work.

When you use a candle, it needs to be new. Never use it for any other purpose once you begin to work with it. If you are working on more than one intention at a time, use different candles.

They may be burned until completely consumed or for a given period of time each day or night. If the ritual calls for the flame to be put out, never blow it out with your breath. You do not need to get complicated or expensive. For instance, I make a cone shape from aluminum foil and place it over the flame to extinguish it. Where your candles are purchased does not matter. You are working with the vibrational energy of the flame and candle.

There are unlimited reasons to use candles. You can bless and banish, attract or repel, protect and aid.

Before you begin, wash your hands first to cleanse metaphysically.

You should wear clean clothes but the type or color is not that important. You may wish to wear the colors of the candles you use to add to the vibration, but it is not necessary.

Use a match, not a lighter, for full strength.

Now you are ready to begin.

CANDLE TYPES AND ATTRACTIONS

Any brand you buy is fine. It doesn't matter which is more expensive or your source of supply. They are all the same.

If you are not sure which to use, then white is best. It covers everything. When you deal with the shapes of the candles, you do so to keep your focus on the intention and because you enjoy doing so. I find there are times I enjoy the visual feedback, especially when working on more than one intention. You may want to try it.

Dave always had trouble when he used a solid colored, tapered candle. He would light the candle and start saying his intention but somewhere in the course of the ritual he would notice that he lost track a little. He had more than one business in motion at the same time, various commitments, and could not stay focused on only one thing at a time. Once he started to use the cat shaped candle (for luck), he no longer had the problem.

Try different methods to see which suits you best at various times. Some of the types and their purpose are listed below:

TYPE	PURPOSE
Cat	
Black	Luck
Green	Money
Red	Love
Image (Shaped as a person)	
Red	Love
Pink	Friends
White	Spirituality, Positivity
Black	Negative
Brown	Losses
Cross or Crucifix	Altar
Seven Knob	Wishes
Reversible	Cancel negative energy
Skull	
Black	Negative
White	Heals
Snake	Protection
Witch	Love
Hand of Glory	Negative
Devil	Evil

Double Action (two layers of colors)

    Black and white   Cleansing, spirituality

    Black and green   Money; luck, success

    Black and red   Love; sex; energy

Triple Action (three color layers)

Red, white, blue   Love; blessing; harmony in your home

Red, white, green   Love, blessing, luck

Seven Day Candles (Stay lit for seven consecutive days)

    Each color has a different meaning. Look under color chart.

CANDLE COLORS

The color of the candle used correlates with the vibrational influence. When you think of money you automatically think of green. If you wish to attract love into your life, the first color you would associate love with would be red. Using the correct color of what you are working on manifesting into your life aids on the vibrational level.

Red   Color of life; will power. Burned for love, sex appeal, sexuality, courage, health, strength, increasing energy levels. Attracts women.

Pink   Color of affection and service; truthfulness. Burned for love, honor, gentleness and Spiritual awakening, diplomacy, success, health.

Red & Pink Attract men.

Orange Color of joy and enthusiasm; prosperity; energy; courage; adaptability. Burned to influence friendships, stimulation, increase mental strength.

Yellow Color of intellect and imagination; invokes spirits; creative; action; cheerfulness; joy; charm; warmth and strength.

Blue Color of balance and abundance. Burned for stability, youthfulness, attracts money, success, luck, healing, fertility, good crops, health, cooperation and generosity.

Brown Color of practicality and solidarity; earthly planes; legal and material levels. Burned for slowing down mental process, balance, thrift, telepathic communication.

Black Color of negativity and depression; un-hexing. Burned for banishing rituals, remembrance and mourning, protection from evil, shield.

Violet   Color of sentimentality and royalty. Burned for tranquillity and sedation.

Purple   Color of luxury and power. Burned for ambition, wisdom, psychic development, draws in spiritual energy, protection, self-esteem, goal attainment, prestige and spirit contact. (Recommended to burn a white candle also.)

Silver   Color of stability; neutrality. Burned for psychic development, remove evil influence, good conquering evil.

Gold   Color of universal brotherhood. Burned for good health, good fortune, intellect, study, teaching, persuasive, universal love.

White   Color of purity; truth; cleanliness; spirituality. Burned for protection, universal color of power and positive vibration, hope, peace, cleansing of a negative atmosphere.

ASTRAL COLORS

The candle color also draws the vibrations of the signs in astrology. When you use these, you can utilize the color to represent yourself (your Sign) or another person (his/her Sign).

ASTROLOGY SIGNS

Aquarius	January 20 to February 18
Pisces	February 19 to March 20
Aries	March 21 to April 20
Taurus	April 21 to May 20
Gemini	May 21 to June 21
Cancer	June 22 to July 22
Leo	July 23 to August 23
Virgo	August 24 to September 23
Libra	September 24 to October 23
Scorpio	October 24 to November 22
Sagittarius	November 23 to December 21
Capricorn	December 22 to January 19

COLOR VIBRATIONAL CONNECTION

ASTRAL CANDLES

Aries — Red symbolizes Aries due to their fiery personalities and their natural leadership abilities. They're

	impatient, proud, ambitious, energetic and impulsive.
Taurus	Blue is a Taurus color because they are cautious and practical. They will always be faithful to their mate, but also very stubborn. They are patient and determined.
Gemini	Yellow is the color of Gemini due to their sensitive nature. They're fickle, restless, imaginative and intelligent.
Cancer	Violet represents Cancer people. They are very emotional, sensitive, quiet and receptive personalities. They are domestic, intuitive and conscientious.
Leo	Is symbolized by Orange because they are optimistic, have personalities that naturally draw things to themselves. They are ambitious, candid, generous and independent.
Virgo	Dark Blue represents Virgo due to their nature which can be thoughtful, very serious, restless, industrious and analytical.
Libra	Green-blue symbolizes Libra. They are harmonious,

balanced, have a sense of justice, are social and creative.

Scorpio   Dark Red symbolizes the passion of Scorpio. They are creative, determined, aggressive and secretive in nature.

Sagittarius Are enterprising, self-reliant people represented by the color Purple. They are idealistic, strong-willed and very giving of themselves.

Capricorn   Dark Green is the color of Capricorn due to their practical and material nature. They are serious, ambitious, persevering and live cautiously.

Aquarius   Their giving and joyful nature is symbolized by the color Bright Blue. They are friendly, intuitive, intelligent and pleasant to be around.

Pisces   Pale Green represents the honest, loving, sympathetic nature of Pisces. They are imaginative, sensitive, idealistic, and an inspiration to others.

DAY AND PLACES

Each candle color vibrates to a day of the week.

DAY	**COLOR**	**PLANET**
Sunday	Gold	Sun
Monday	Silver	Moon
Tuesday	Red	Mars
Wednesday	Yellow	Mercury
Thursday	Green	Jupiter
Friday	Pink	Venus
Saturday	Deep Blue	Saturn

PLANETARY DAYS AND HOURS - ACTIVITIES

The best days to start certain activities are as follows:

Sun — Obtaining wealth; gaining favor; making friends; success; career; promotion; cardiac difficulties; fame; dealing with authoritative figures; dealing with children; health; healing; entertainment; speculation and risk; Divine Power.

Moon — Voyages; messages; conception and fertility; love; family; home; psychic development; dealing with the public; intuition; dreams; clairvoyance; property dealings; nutrition; change; sleep; wells and streams; the sea.

Mars   Protection from physical and psychical dangers; courage; strength; operations; surgery; pain; health; conflict; (male) endurance; adventure; fever; ambition; leadership; overcoming obstacles; aggression; working with machinery; new ventures; self-interests; avoidance of violence and anger; arrivals.

Mercury   Brothers and sisters; business; apparitions; writing; neighbors; dealing with the mind; overcoming distress; communications; self-improvement; divination; analysis; predictions; dealing with documents; visits and visitors; skills involving manual dexterity.

Jupiter   Burn for prosperity (expansion); gambling; opening the mind to new philosophical concepts; higher education; publications and publishers; insurance dealings; money; legal matters; dealing with grandchildren; luck; obtaining honors; preserving health; materialism; promoting dreams; ceremonies; mediumistic matters; spiritualism; the psychic areas; hospital dealings; prison dealings; charitable work; all illusionary things.

Venus	Love; travel; (female) harmony; marriage; art; beauty; musical; making friends; pleasure; social events; artistic events; money; investments; contracts; agreements; niece and nephew dealings.

Saturn	Termination; matters of houses; property; Karma; responsibility; reincarnation; career; fame; fate; employment; development of inventions (especially electrical, nuclear or space technology); divorce dealings; separations; fears; wishes; friends; dealing with son-in-laws; daughters; possessions; causing good or ill fortune to business; goods acquiring learning.

TIMING OF RITUALS

MOON PHASE	PURPOSE
New moon	To bring something in.
Waxing Moon (new to full)	To increase; vitalize; put into motion.
Full moon	High point of energy. It worked up to fulfillment.
Waning moon (full to new)	To decrease or banish.

Perform for the same purpose as the planetary influences.

PLANET

Solar Ritual	Initiated on Sunday, performed for one-four days with a Gold candle.
Lunar Ritual	Initiated on Monday, performed for two-seven days with a Silver candle.
Martian Ritual	Initiated on Tuesday, performed for nine days with a Red candle.
Mercurial Ritual	Initiated on Wednesday, performed for five days with a Yellow candle.
Jupiterian Ritual	Initiated on Thursday, performed for three days with a Green candle.
Venusian Ritual	Initiated on Friday, performed for six days with a Pink candle.
Saturnian Ritual	Initiated on Saturday, performed for eight days with a Deep Blue candle.

YOUR PERSONAL DAY FOR CANDLEBURNING

Find your best (or personal) day. When you burn your candle, it will pick up your own level of abilities. So if your personal day is #1 and you want to start on a self-improvement course, wait two more days. On your personal #3 day you would get the full benefit of the vibrational energies.

To find which is your personal day, use the following formula:

Add:	Your month of birth
+	Your day of birth
+	Present month
+	Present day
+	Present year

Reduce the total to one digit.

The following is an example. Substitute your own birth date and the current date to determine your own personal day.

Example: Birth Date: 10-18-1948. Today is 2-16-1988.

Add:	10
+	18
+	2
+	16
+	1988

$$2034 = 2 + 0 + 3 + 4 = 9$$

Thus, your personal day would be #9.

PERSONAL DAY

#1 Personal Day

I suggest burning a *Red* candle.

The activities that are best suited for this day are:

Interviews	Sports
Acquire a raise	Beginning anything
Making important change	Following hunches
Selling ideas to others	Being creative and artistic
Entering contests	Taking leisure walks

#2 Personal Day

I suggest burning a *Silver* candle.

The activities that are best for this day are:

Being receptive listener	Starting hobbies
Express love and charm	Working on relationships
Being tactful	Making marriage proposals
Learning others' views	Taking a scenic drive
Being charitable	Partnership

#3 Personal Day

I suggest burning a *Yellow* candle.

The activities that are best for this day are:

      Avoiding gossip and worry   Communications
      Shopping sprees   Self-improvement
      Remodeling   Self-expression
      All social gatherings   Gift buying
      Short trips   Writing
      Creativity

#4 Personal Day

I suggest burning a *Green* candle.

The activities that are best for this day are:

      Building toward future   Paying attention to health
      Signing contracts   Cleaning
      Partnerships   Taking inventory
      Fixing up the house   Thrift
      Practicality

#5 Personal Day

I suggest burning an *Orange* candle.

The activities that are best for this day are:

Originality	Planning social events
Changes	Romantic interests
Getting enjoyment	Sports
Short trips	New friendships
Decisions	

#6 Personal Day

I suggest burning a *Blue* candle.

The activities that are best for this day are:

Repaying debts, calls	Harmony
Remodeling the home	Meeting responsibilities
Appreciating family	Visiting the sick
Making marriage proposal	Family gatherings
Making marriage plans	Dealing with intellect

#7 Personal Day

I suggest burning a *Purple* candle.

The activities that are best for this day are:

> Studying the psychic, spirituality   Decision making
> Meditation   Future plans
> Consulting authority figures
> Avoiding negative atmospheres
> Seeing doctors, lawyers and dentists

#8 Personal Days

I suggest burning a *Brown* candle.

The activities that are best for this day are:

> Taking care of business   Loaning money
> Paying debts   Expressing self-reliance
> Asking for a raise   Interviews
> Patience and practicality Being charitable
> Reviewing finances   Material dealings

#9 Personal Day

I suggest burning a *Gold* candle.

The activities that are best for this day are:

Settling debts	Being charitable
Studying the psychic & occult	Making public appearances
Writing letters	Self-expression
Being creative	New friendship
Entertaining friends	Eliminating old ideas
Finishing up old projects	Ending negative situations

FIXING THE CANDLE

To anoint (or dress) a candle, you should use the oils which vibrate to what you are working on. Focus on your intention as you do this.

Work with a new candle. Take off the old vibration by cleansing it with soap and water. If it is in a glass, clean the glass in the same manner, drying it with a paper towel. Put your own vibration on the candle when you dress it.

Next, bless it with a prayer, any prayer with which you feel positive.

An example: I ask for Thy blessing on this candle, which I use in the name of the Father, the Son, and the Holy Spirit. Thank you, Father.

As you make your petition, *see* it, *feel* it, *know* it will happen.

Your basic intention, such as a person's name, or the amount of money needed, should be written on the candle with something sharp. Try to fit it on the bottom. Make the pentagram (five pointed star) on the bottom with the wick being in the middle. Never break contact from the candle when you do this. If you do, just start again at the bottom left point.

Next, take two or three drops of the oil and rub the candle with it from the center toward the top, including the tip of the wick, then from the center toward the bottom.

If you use a Seven Day Candle (or any candle in a glass), make the pentagram on the top and rub the oil to the tip of the wick. Another method is from the bottom to the tip.

When attracting things to you, hold the candle so the wick is toward you and put the oil on, rubbing it toward you.

To repel, point the wick away from your body and rub the oil from the candle bottom to the wick away from you.

CANDLE FORMULAE

There are many altar rituals. However, you can use the following formulae. They are simplified, direct and with full Power.

UNHEXING

Start on a Wednesday.

Use a black candle and two green candles, one on each side of the black candle.

Anoint these with Uncrossing Oil.

Burn High John incense for seven days.

Light the candles for five minutes every night.

While the candles burn, pray Psalm #10. Do this until the black candle is all gone.

PROPHECY

Use a tapered white candle.

Bless the room you are working in through the name and power of the Father, the Son, and the Holy Spirit.

Burn Frankincense.

Next, focus your gaze on the candle flame. In a short while you will "see" people, objects, scenery, or just "know" -- whatever way, the information is coming in to you.

WISHES

Burn a Seven Knob candle, one Knob each day, and concentrate on your wishes. Or you can burn each knob for seven different intentions.

You can use a Seven Day candle in the same manner by sectioning it off for the seven days.

TO OVERCOME AN ENEMY

Burn a Seven Day white candle and a black tapered candle. Do this for two consecutive weeks.

Start on a Sunday (for success).

Burn the black candle for ten minutes a night and repeat the following:

In the name of the Christ and through the Power,
I am shielded from all that is harmful.
Negativity now goes back to its sender,
My life turns around to positive only.
So Be It.

LOVE

Burn a red candle every night at sunset, ten minutes a night, until it is gone. Say once when you light the candle:

Red candle, red candle, let this offering to you help bring my Lover (name) to me alone and forever more.

Then repeat it when you put the candle out.

NEW LOVE

If a person wants a lover, but there isn't anyone in particular, or if the person is looking for someone new, always substitute the word "partner" for the name.

LOVE ATTRACTION

Burn a red candle every night until the candle is gone. Do this for five minutes at a time. Concentrate on the person that you want and say:

(Fill in the Name) is the one I want, through Divine Power,
in a Perfect Way, for now and forever.
As this Light burns, so dies (his or her) desire burn for me,
and only I can fulfill this desire.
So Be It.

LOVE SPELL

Anoint a red candle with Love oil.
Say the incantation for five nights in a row.
Repeat three times:

I am possessed by love that is burning for (name) and
I want (name) to have this same burning for me and me only.
Let this come from Spirit and enter (name).
Let (name) desire me as never before.
(Name) must feel this same feeling as I feel.
Spirit of the Air and Fire let (name) burn for me
and not rest until we are together.
So Be It.

BRING MONEY IN

Use a green Seven Day Candle.

Place a silver dime or nickel in the bottom of the glass.

Write your petition on parchment paper and fold it in thirds using the following method: First, fold the top of the paper down, then turn it upside down and repeat the process so you have the thirds completed.

Place the parchment on top of the coins in the glass.

Sprinkle one teaspoon of sugar to sweeten it.

Sprinkle one-half teaspoon of Gold Dust on top of the sugar.

Dress the candle with High John oil.

Carve three dollar signs {$$$} on the sides of the candle.

Place the candle in the glass.

Carve a spiral on the top, starting from the edge to the wick.

Pour eight drops of Money Oil onto the top of the candle.

Sprinkle 1/4 teaspoon sugar and 1/4 teaspoon Gold Dust on top.

Place the candle in the center of a white bowl.

Each night place some small change into the bowl. Visualize your money supply growing.

Works within two weeks.

TO WIN IN COURT

Use a black candle.

Write your petition in black ink on parchment paper.

Dress the candle with High John The Conqueror Oil.

Fold the parchment paper in half, folding it away from your body.

Place it under the candle in the glass. Light it.

Burn Seven African Powers incense and visualize a favorable outcome in court dealings.

Make plans for what you will be doing after the court date.

Visualize it to give it force. After all, if you are going on a vacation, you cannot be in jail.

IMPROVING BUSINESS

Use a piece of green colored cloth.

Two gold candles and one green candle.

Dress the candles with High John The Conqueror Oil.

Place the green candle in the middle of a white bowl.

Place the two gold candles on each side of the green candle on the cloth.

In a bowl, sprinkle:
- 1/2 teaspoon sugar
- 1/4 teaspoon Gold Dust
- 1/4 teaspoon Silver Dust

Pray Psalm #114 each night.

SPIRITUALITY

Burn a Double Action candle of purple and white.

Add your Personal Day candle.

Burn Frankincense and Myrrh for twenty minutes a night.

During this time, pray this affirmation:

He is, I am, We are One.

Visualize the bright white light from above your head, down through your Crown Chakra and to your Heart Chakra.

Feel it, see it or know that we are One with God as co-creators.

FINANCIAL GAIN

Anoint a green candle and your Personal Day candle with Money Oil.

Write the amount of money needed on a piece of parchment paper in black ink.

Fold it in half and place it underneath your Personal Day candle.

Light the candles for twenty minutes per day and see your money coming to you for your needs. Know that it is there. As you ask, so shall you be answered.

SUCCESS

Anoint three orange candles with Success Oil. Place them in a row three inches apart.

Write your petition for success on parchment paper in black ink.

Place it under the middle candle.

Burn High John The Conqueror incense.

Allow twenty minutes for this work, and use this incantation:

Through Divine Power In a Perfect Way,
Success comes to me in every way,
Bring Success for it is mine,
Success in (fill in your need) is very high,
As I "know" this is, so shall it be,
Success flows easily and abundantly to me.
So Be It!
Thank You, Father.

OBTAINING MONEY

Anoint five green candles, your Personal Day candle, and your Astral candle with Money Drawing Oil.

Carve two dollar signs {$$} on each side of all the candles.

Place the Personal Day candle and Astral candle next to each other.

Place the five green candles in a row behind these.

Light them and use the following incantation:

> As the flames of the candles,
> Seek to grow higher,
> So money comes to me,
> Through desire.
> Let this money come to me NOW,
> Through Air and Earth,
> Through Water and Fire,
> No power of man,
> Blocks what I aspire.
> So Be It!
> Thank You, Father.

Whatever you put your thoughts into, you manifest. Robert used this method to achieve his goal:

He needed $2,000.00 for a car. He put some money down on the car, then put all his thoughts into the work every night, knowing the money would be there when he needed it.

The time came when he had three days left to either pay for the car which had been on hold for him or let it go back on the market.

Two days prior to the deadline Robert had a new construction job offer. He decided to take it and received in advance more than half of the money needed for the car. The balance of the money for the job was to be paid upon completion of the work.

Still he didn't have enough. He kept the ritual going.

On the day he needed to go for the car, he received an envelope in the mail. An old friend repaid a long-forgotten debt. This sum was ten dollars over the amount he needed.

Even when the money does not come in the way you expect, it still comes.

Always remember to thank God when the supply comes in, to acknowledge the source, and keep the flow moving.

OVERCOME OBSTACLES

Use a Personal Day candle and anoint it with High John Oil.

Burn this each night for fifteen minutes and affirm:

>All my paths are cleared,
>I walk with God.

HAPPINESS

Burn your Personal Day candle and an orange candle.

Anoint these with Success Oil.

Pray Psalm #126.

Use Rose or Sandalwood incense.

LUCK

Anoint a green candle, an orange candle, and a white candle with Fast Luck Oil.

Place the green candle in the middle, the white candle on the right, and the orange candle on the left.

Burn Jasmine incense.

On parchment paper, write:

Life flows easily to me.
Everything I touch turns to gold.
In the name of Divine Power.
So Be It!

Place this under the green candle, folded in half.

Do this ritual for fifteen minutes each night.

CHAPTER SEVEN

UNLOCKING THE SECRETS OF LOVE POTIONS

Occult Grimoire & Magical Formulary A Workbook For Creating A Positive Life

UNLOCKING THE SECRETS OF LOVE POTIONS

Love potions are concoctions which have a high rate of attracting someone into your life. When the person drinks the potion, it will make her or him more amorous.

Potions have been used since ancient times as another form of magic. part of the positive results are due to the Power of the Word, or Thought.

When you blend the love potion, concentrate on your intentions. Decide prior to starting what it is that you want as the result. This will link the petitioner to the aspect of the universal mind, and telepathically set a trigger off in the mind of the one desired.

The potion at the time of the blending will pull the energy force into culmination.

There are many formulae for love potions. Try a few to decide your preference.

There are love potions sold commercially though not advertised as such. Their effectiveness is due to the vibrational influences.

Sloe Gin	A liqueur from the sloe berry. Also known as blackthorn. This is an old ingredient added to love potions.
May Wine	This is flavored with woodruff. It is a sweet White wine.

Drambuie	A liqueur consisting of a base of Scotch malt whiskey. Also has honey and spices.
Metaxa	Greek resinous dark, sweet liqueur. It has a base of brandy.
Advokaat	An egg and brandy liqueur.
Chartreuse	A French liqueur. It is said that the secret formula contains one hundred and thirty varied herbs and spices.
Vermouth	This wine contains most of the barks and herbs used in the old love potions. One of the ingredients is *Wermut*, meaning "essence of man", thus the name *Vermouth*.
Mazcal	A liqueur consisting of a brandy base with cherries, peaches, crushed seeds of apricots, plums, and orange flavoring. Tastes of almonds.
Kümmel	A German liqueur. Consists of seeds, one of them being caraway seeds.

You can also make your own love potions. Some of these potions may be used to help promote a relationship with one special person; others can be prepared in volume to be used at a party.

HYPOCRAS APHRODISIAQUE

1 oz. ginger
1 oz. crushed cinnamon bark
1/3 oz. clove
1 2/3 pts. red table wine

Let this mixture macerate for five days. Strain through a cloth, using a funnel to make pouring easier.

Add one ounce of this blend to the wine that is normally served.

ELFIN SPIRITS

1/5 vodka - Pour into a jar.
Bring the following to a boil:
    1 two oz. jar of instant coffee
    1 Vanilla bean
    1 small container of sesame seeds
    1/2 oz. Mandrake root
    1 lb. granulated sugar
Add to the vodka.

Let this macerate for one month. Stir every day. Leave a cover on the jar. Strain.

SYRUP OF PRIAPUS

1/2 oz. flowers of stoeches

2/3 oz. wild carrots

25 myrtle berries

50 dried dates

2/3 oz. anise

4 egg yolks

1/2 oz. saffron flowers

1 pt. pure spring water

Warm the ingredients in an earthen or cast iron pot with a lid for twenty-five minutes. Filter it through a cloth.

Add two ounces of pure honey.

Let it macerate twenty-four hours. Shake and pass through a sieve.

Serve one or two teaspoons at night.

LIQUEUR OF LOVE

Put the following ingredients in a wine glass:

1/2 glass of maraschino

1 yellow of an egg

1/4 glass Creme de Cocao

1/4 glass Madeira

1/4 glass brandy

Do not mix. Leave the egg yolk whole.

SWEET PASSION

Place these ingredients in a glass:

4 drops Curacao

4 lumps of sugar

1 wine glass of red Port wine

Fill a glass with mixture, warm it almost to a boil. Serve this with a lemon with four cloves through it. Add a pinch of grated nutmeg.

TIGER LUST

Utilized for the purpose of stamina in a male. Stimulator.

Fill 3/4 of an 8 oz. glass with Guinea Stout

Add 3 teaspoons sweet condensed milk

1 raw egg

Beat and drink this immediately. it is to be taken thirty to forty-five minutes before becoming intimate.

EYE OF THE GIANT

For non-alcohol users. Same results on a power level as the previous one.

    Fill 3/4 of an 8 oz. glass with milk
    1 banana
    1 raw egg
    3 teaspoons honey (or to taste)
    a few raisins (optional)

Blend these together. Drink immediately. To be taken thirty to forty-five minutes before intimacy.

This can be drunk before and after if you want to reproduce the effect.

I had a client who was very happily married. However, her love relation was not of the intensity she and her husband desired. They decided to use this formula. Within two weeks she called to let me know it works on a power level and if anything, they may need to tone down.

GENTIAN WINE

Add 1 oz. of grated gentian roots to 3 1/2 pts. brandy and a little wine. Macerate for twenty-four hours.

Put a lid on the jar. Leave it in the sun for eight days. Filter this before drinking.

DRAGON WINE

Boil the following ingredients:
- 16 oz. red wine
- 5 cinnamon sticks

Drink while it is still warm.

SEXUAL POWER

- 1 oz. Shizandra Chinesis
- 2 oz. Epimedium Macranthum
- 1 oz. Boswellia Glabra
- 1 oz. Ginseng
- 1 1/2 oz. Cistanche Salsa
- 1 1/2 oz. Mantis Cocoon
- 1 oz. Snidium Monnieri
- 2 oz. Cynomorium Coccineum
- 1 oz. Polygala Tenuifolia (Siberian Mugwort - sends Chi to the heart.)

Blend and boil. Drink for vitality.

WINE OF THE WIZARD

Incorporate the following into a fifth of white wine:

- 1 oz. Cinnamon bark
- 2 Vanilla beans
- 1 oz. Rhubarb
- 1 oz. Ginseng

Macerate for two weeks. Stir daily. Filter and drink.

WINE OF THE SWORD

Bring the following substances to a boil:

- 16 oz. Red wine
- a few cloves

Drink this while still warm.

SWORD OF POWER

- 1/2 oz. Prince ginseng
- a few cinnamon pieces

Make an infusion. Let stand until it is not too hot to drink.

Drink it with the one you desire and focus on your intention.

GOBLIN JUICE

This is very good to use at a party as a punch. It is not on as high a power level as those mentioned above.

Add together these ingredients:

- 1/5 Rum
- 1/5 Vodka
- 1 lg. can of pineapple-grapefruit drink
- 1 small can frozen orange juice
    - (diluted as instructed on container)
- 4 oz. Grenadine

Serve this with ice and have fun.

Love potions have power and are used as a strong force when utilized for the good of all persons concerned.

Try some of these potions and discover which one you like the best.

CHAPTER EIGHT

MYSTICAL INCENSE

Occult Grimoire & Magical Formulary A Workbook For Creating A Positive Life

MYSTICAL INCENSE

Incense was and still is utilized by Grecians, Romans, Indians and numerous others.

Incense sets up certain vibrational levels and has its place in rituals, but itself as an attracting force, and even by the uninitiated for its aroma.

Incense is used in worship in the temples of China, Tibet, India, and in Christian churches, to name a few.

Beliefs concerning the use of incense are many and varied. Some believe it drives away evil forces. Others use incense to call in Spirit. It is used on the altar as an offering to God. Its purpose may be to enhance a ceremonial ritual such as a wedding, funeral, feast, birth, etc. Incense may be burned to attract love, to help in out-of-body travel or used for defense.

There aren't any limits as to who burns incense. It is used by spiritualists, occultists, psychics, business men, healers, lovers, ministers, and homemakers.

The Bible contains many instances. The Three Wise Men brought Frankincense and Myrrh to the Christ Child. It is also mentioned in Leviticus 16:12-13.

Incense may be purchased in various forms - sticks, cones or powder, or you may choose to make your own.

If you do prepare your own incense, burn the spice or substance on self-igniting charcoal.

VIBRATIONAL INFLUENCES

Incense	Purpose
Cinnamon	Tones down arguments in your home. Use it when your negative relatives come to visit. They will argue when they leave, but they'll get along in your home. Promotes a giving nature.
Peach	Good for social atmosphere. If you are worried about how a guest will act, this will keep the person on a more appropriate behavioral level.
Allspice	Comfortable party environment.
Orange	Calm. Productive.
Lemon	To clarify. Stimulate.
Carnation	Healing. Tone down emotional and mental disruptions.
Rose	Love, Prophecy, Spiritual. To quiet down.

Chrysanthemum	Nourishing atmosphere. Mothering.
Frankincense	Success. Bless. Cleanse. Call in highest level of Spirit.
Myrrh	Never burn by itself. Always use with Frankincense. Makes the contact on a Spirit level. Without Frankincense you may summon negative influences on the astral plane by mistake. Myrrh makes the contact. Frankincense keeps it on the Highest plane.
Jasmine	Calmness on your mental plane. Mental clarity.
Sandalwood	High spiritual vibration. Calming. Luck.
Pine	Health. Times of need.
Patchouli	Love. To attract and inspire.
High John the Conqueror	Success on all levels.
Lavender	Love. Money. Harmony.

Adam and Eve	Attracts and helps hold love.
Wisteria	Luck.
Peaceful Home	Halts bad feelings.
Astrological (each sign has its own incense: Aries, etc.)	Burned by those born under that particular Zodiac sign.
Seven African Powers	Brings in Finance. Protects. Light it and say the names of the 7 Voodoo deities: Chango. Ochun. Yemala. Obatia. Ogun. Orula. Elequa.
Stay At Home	Stops infidelity. Increases marital bliss.
Uncrossing	Cancel hex or curse.
Van Van	Good luck and Power.
Venus	Love.

San Jude	Helps difficult situations. Peace.
Power	Heightens your rituals. Add to other incense or use by itself.
Lucky Plant	Love. Money.
Money Drawing	Finance.
Master	Heightens ritual.
House Blessing	Protection. Purifies.
Dove's Blood	Peace. Harmony.
Dragon Blood	Powerful. Luck. Protection.
Bingo	Luck to play.
Fast Luck	Fast results.
Altar	Blessings. Spirit help.
Tobacco	Protection.
Temple	Ceremonies. Spirituality. Answered Prayers.

Incense has been used as an offering to God. Utilize it at the time of invocation in rituals, such as with voodoo.

It may be used as an aid in times of stress, and to keep things moving in a positive way when there aren't any problems.

There isn't any set time to work with incense. You can use it once a day, a few times a day, or just when the need arises.

The Tibetan monks carry incense as part of an amulet they wear.

I have found Oriental incense gives off a soothing fragrance that helps me to relax, especially prior to meditation or when working in a spiritual state.

You need to try several types to find which ones fit you. When you've had a hard day at work, it is a perfect time to burn incense. Some incense is soothing and calming to you and allows you to unwind easily.

Any form of incense you choose to use has a vibration unto itself. Follow the formulae as they are given to achieve the best results.

INCENSE FORMULAE

FOR CONCENTRATION

Add together:
- 1/4 teaspoon alum
- 3 teaspoons mace

Helps concentration. I burn it to help my children when they do homework. Use it when studying for an exam.

QUIETING EFFECT

Burn *Rose* incense when children go to bed to quiet active vibrations in the room.

HEAVIEST CLEANSING METHOD

1/8 teaspoon *Dragon Blood* incense

Place on top of self-igniting charcoal.

Open windows and REMOVE yourself and pets, as it is very strong.

After burning *Dragon Blood*, next burn *Frankincense*.

FAST MONEY

Burn Pure:

Sandalwood

Frankincense

Myrrh

Concentrate on money coming to you NOW.

FINANCE

Carry *Sandalwood* and Charcoal with you at all times.

UN-HEX

Burn *Dragon Blood* incense for seven nights in a row.
Do this at midnight.

Carry a piece of it at all times.

LOVE

Write your petition on a piece of parchment paper.

Place it under the *Rose* incense.

Light the incense and repeat seven times:

As the smoke begins to rise,
So does (Fill in the name of the person you want) desire start,
As it reaches up to God,
So does (Fill in his/her name) become mine.

Do this every night until you get your desire.

Remember, we only bring the person in. Once there, you have to work at your relationship on a normal level to keep it going.

POSITIVE HOME

Burn *John The Conqueror* and make sure you have the scent in every room. This will send away negativity and protect your home. It will insure that people entering your home will be more positive than they might otherwise have been.

At times my boys, Rob and Rick, have brought friends home who were negative, so I burned *John The Conqueror* incense. It did not change the personalities of the negative friends, but they did tone down and eventually found other friends. Thus, the way was opened for more positive friends to come into my boys' lives.

FAST BUSINESS

Write your petition on parchment paper.

Place it under *Money Drawing* incense.

Place two green Lodestones next to it, one on each side of the incense. As you light it, repeat eight times:

> My business rises higher and higher,
> As does this smoke strive to aspire,
> Money flows to me easily,
> Business grows consistently.

After the 8th time, end it with:

In the name of the Father, Son and Holy Spirit. Thank you. It is done NOW.

A business man came to me a few years ago because he needed to increase his business. He just opened an auto body shop and things were moving very slowly. If it kept going in the same way, he would be unable to afford to keep his shop open.

He was very good in his work and dealt with all his customers honestly. He used the above method and very soon more customers started coming in, thus bringing in the money he needed to stay in business. As his good reputation spread by word of mouth, his business increased even more.

FORMULAE TO GET A NEW JOB

Before you leave your house to look for a job, burn a green candle anointed with *Success Oil* for twenty minutes each day.

Burn *John The Conqueror* incense. Buy it in the bag. Concentrate as you light it on what type of job you want, on your desires regarding your work.

Do this until the job comes in.

I find in many cases that I prefer to work with the powdered incense. It lasts longer when burned - about fifteen to twenty minutes when two teaspoons are used.

MAGNET ATTRACTIONS

Place the incense burner over two pieces of lodestone.
Burn *Frankincense* in the room you are occupying.
Do this in the hour of the break of dawn.

Mystics use this method to tune into the magnetic energy flow of nature surrounding the earth. It is felt that the positive vibrations will be attracted to you. Also, the energies magnetize you so that you will be able to help others more.

SPIRIT HELPERS

Burn *Frankincense* for the aroma and request your intention.

Have a glass of water with one teaspoon of sea salt added to it and next to the candle. This will help keep you tuned to positive spirit.

Incense has been used to contact Spirit helpers for centuries.

Always give thanks for their aid in the name of God.

PSYCHIC VIBRATIONS

You can burn any form of incense in conjunction with seeking insight.

The incense can heighten the consciousness of the psychic.

The smoke also may have a calming result.

PROTECTION

When any incense is burned it will disintegrate the negative vibrations within its range.

You can burn as much incense as you desire.

TO INCREASE OPPORTUNITY

Burn *Cinnamon* and *Clove* in a dry powder form over self-igniting coal.

It will multiply your success and make it easier to succeed in your endeavors.

HARMONY

Burn *Ginger* in a powdered form.

Do this especially in areas where the most arguments occur.

PROPHECY

Over self-igniting coal, use *Benzoin*.

Close your eyes and sit relaxed.

Note the information coming in. It may come as a vision, sound or any other form.

SEEKING SPIRIT AID

May be done by burning *Sandalwood*. (Note: This ritual also may be performed without incense.)

Close your eyes and relax.

Stand with your feet slightly apart. Hold your hands down at your sides but not touching them.

Take a deep breath and as you inhale, say to yourself:

> I bring the Universal Forces into my Body.
> I ask for Protection, Truth and Guidance.

Let yourself exhale. Repeat this seven times.

Next, make your petition. If you cannot use exact wording, state your problem and request a solution.

Then cross your arms across your chest. (To shut down.)

Repeat "Thank you, Father" three times.

Open your eyes. Know that you are helped.

Give yourself a few minutes to listen within. If you get information, ACT on it.

If you get a first impression to do something concerning what you petitioned, ACT on it. You are being guided.

TO ATTRACT LOVE

Burn *Rose* incense for five nights.

Light it and as it burns each night, use the following invocation:

> Hear me, Venus, Spirit of Love,
> I desire to excite love in the heart of (name).
> Use they Power to bring my desire to me 1,000 fold,
> In a Perfect Way.
> I conjure this command, Venus.
> So Be It.
> Thank You, Father.

FINANCE

Burn three green candles in a row, anointed with *Money Oil*.

Burn *Sandalwood* or *Money* incense. Place it in front of the middle candle.

Use the following invocation:

> I command thee, Sachiel,
> To do my bidding,
> Bring the money I need ($ amount),

Immediately and in a Perfect Way.
It flows to me NOW.
I command it thus, Sachiel.
So Be It.
Thank You.

Do this each night at 8:00 p.m. for eight days.

COURT

Burn *High John The Conqueror* incense each night for seven nights before court.

As you light it, repeat seven times:

As above,
So below,
As this smoke rises,
So does any negative outcome go with it.
As it rises,
It grants my desires,
So Be It.
Thank You, Lord.

Then visualize the outcome you want. "See" yourself leaving the court happy and free.

RAISE AND JOB PROMOTION

Burn *Seven African Power* incense each night for eight nights.

Carry *St. John's* herb with you at all times (especially to your job).

Do not ask for a raise or promotion on a Monday.

Do not buy stocks on this day. (Moon is in Scorpio.)

CLEANSE HOME

Place a glass of water between two white candles.

Light *Tobacco* incense or *Sandalwood*.

Say The Lord's Prayer.

Go to each corner of the room with the incense and in each corner say:

> This House is Blessed in the Name of the Father,
> Son and Holy Spirit.

When you are through, go outside and throw the water away from the house.

LOST OBJECTS

If you lost an object, burn *Wisteria* incense.

Look into the smoke and make your request, asking to be shown where your missing object is.

Give it a few minutes and you will see the answer in the smoke.

Or you will remember it.

SMUDGING

A Native American Indian ritual.

A special plant is burned in the area where they will be working.

Although not technically used as incense, it can be utilized in much the same way prior to ceremonies, healing, spiritual teachings, etc.

When burned (usually *sage*), the smoke is fanned through the entire area from each cardinal point. This cleanses and protects from negativity. Some Indians use a feather to disperse the smoke.

As an honorary member of the Tuscarora tribe, I find this method very strong.

CHAPTER NINE

CRYSTALS AND STONES A SOURCE OF POWER

Occult Grimoire & Magical Formulary A Workbook For Creating A Positive Life

CRYSTALS AND STONES

A SOURCE OF POWER

In my first book, Psychic Vibrations of Crystals, Gems and Stones, I discussed the use of their power at higher levels of consciousness and their enhancement of psychic abilities. For those who missed my book, I enclose this chapter.

Crystals and stones are one of the most ancient metaphysical tools. In times past, these stones were used full force, in a direct way, and produced positive results. More recently complicated methods have been devised buy I find the less complicated the tool, the less the results are toned down.

Stones and their influences are an exact science. The vibrations are utilized for varied reasons - spiritual, emotional, mental and physical. The same stone may have varied effects on different people, depending on each person's vibration. It should be noted that to see the results would take time.

We are coming full circle and rediscovering the ancient sciences, the "lost arts". Actually, this treasured information was never totally lost but was carefully preserved by a select few. At times, due to the political atmosphere, the information simply went underground.

Stones have been in use for numerous reasons from the ancient times right up to the present. First, because they *do* work and secondly, they have been valued for their durability, color and financial worth.

Stones have a physical vibration. Due to this, they attract other vibrations that are in their vicinity thus heightening our sensitivity. They can send out their vibrations thereby influencing our physical bodies or environment.

There are legends surrounding many of the stones, such as the one associated with the mineral called Staurolite. This has also been called Baelar Taufstein or Baptismal Stone and is known for its use as an amulet at baptism. Staurolite is also called Fairy Cross. They are formed in that shape by nature, and when mined, look like a cross. There are many stories associated with this stone. One of the most poignant legends is that of fairies playing by a spring when a messenger elf came and told them about the crucifixion of Christ. The fairies were so sad that they cried, each tear turning into the form of the cross - the crystal we know as the Fairy Cross.

According to the legends, the Quartz Crystals were considered magical stones. They were utilized for divination, healing, high energy, telepathy, protection, for memory storage, attracting needs, controlling nature's forces, and much more.

Among mystics these stones were called "the Philosopher's stone".

The clear Quartz Crystal is used for crystal gazing. It gives a positive focus. The Quartz Crystal is said to be the stone used by Merlin as a source of knowledge.

Another form of quartz is known as the Amethyst. The lore tells us that the God Bacchus was offended by what he felt was neglect and decided to avenge himself. He said that the first person he met would be eaten by tigers.

The first to come along was a mortal maiden named Amethyst, very beautiful and pure of heart. She was going to her place of worship to pray to the Goddess Diana.

When the tigers attacked, she prayed to Diana for help. Diana turned her into a white stone to protect her.

Bacchus repented upon seeing this and poured wine over Amethyst as an atonement, turning the stone to its beautiful color. Ever since, it is said when wearing an Amethyst you will not be able to get drunk. It tones down the effect.

Amethyst is also known for creating alertness, keeping peace, raising the intellect and helping to gain knowledge.

As a mystic, I find certain gifts from nature are a source of Power. Being aware of this, we should put to work what God has given us.

The powers of these crystals and stones are unlimited. You can carry them anywhere on your person or wear them as jewelry. It will not be obvious to others that you are "working". They can be an elixir or a talisman; bring protection or a prediction. The stones have more than one purpose and so need to be utilized properly.

As an example, Quartz Crystal would be your choice for any of the following: protection, healing, sending of energy, telepathy, materialization, dematerialization, memory storage, for rain-making by medicine men, prophecy.

As you can see, it is vital to know how to achieve the best results from each stone at its higher ability level. The following formulae will give you this aid.

CLEANSING THE STONES

Prior to working with stones, they should be cleansed in order to remove any negative energy. You want to work only with positive energy. The energy attached may be from the atmosphere of the place you bought it, or it may have belonged to a negative person or even the people who mined it may have had negative vibrations.

There are several methods for cleansing but these are the two I find most effective:

Place the stones in a glass or bowl of water to which a little sea salt has been added. Leave in direct sunlight for three days. You do not need to have this outside. It can be placed on a table or anywhere that it will not be touched by others.

If you have a strong awareness of the God Energy within us all, simply hold the stones in your hand. Then Bless them through the Name and Power of God.

Now you are ready to go to work.

HELP IN MEDITATION

Prior to meditation, place the stones in the following pattern:
Form a triangle of stones.
Stand a terminated clear Quartz Crystal, pointing up, in the center of the triangle of stones.
At the left tip of the base of the triangle, place an Azurite.
At the right tip of the base of the triangle, place a Rose Quartz.

Then cup your hands on both sides of this layout, palms toward the stones.

Close your eyes and begin your meditation in a comfortable sitting position.

MEDITATION AID

Lie down on your back in a comfortable position prior to meditation. Place the stones in their proper alignment as follows:

Clear large Quartz Crystal with termination on one end - place on navel pointing toward the feet.

Clear smaller Quartz Crystal with termination on one end - place between solar plexus and Heart Chakra.

Raw Rose Quartz - place over Heart Chakra.

Raw Adventurine stone - place over Throat Chakra.

Raw Amethyst - pace over the Third Eye Chakra.

Close your eyes and meditate.

LOVE ATTRACTION

Wrap a Moonstone in a piece of yellow material and give it to the one you love to carry. This will keep your mate closer.

It is best to exchange if you are in a long term or marriage relationship.

INFIDELITY

To stop this, place a John The Conqueror root and a Moonstone under the person's pillow at night when you go to bed together. It will make the lover true to you.

Repeat to yourself: Through Divine Power, this man/woman will only be with me, and in a Perfect Way. Now and Always.

So Be It.

LOVE - VERY POWERFUL

The night of the full moon, concentrate on what you desire. Write this down on a piece of paper with the name of the one you desire on it. Use red ink on white paper. Dove's Blood Ink is best, on parchment paper. Fold the paper and light it with an Emerald stone placed next to it. Burn the paper in an ashtray or where convenient. While it is burning, concentrate very strongly on what you want NOW and in a Perfect Way.

When you are done, throw the ashes outside to the wind.

Take the Emerald and carry it with you until you get your results.

HEALTH

Carry a Red Jasper to help speed up your natural healing process. Stay on a healthier level.

MONEY ATTRACTION

During a full moon, place a Turquoise stone in its direct light - in front of your window is fine.

The next morning, place the stone in a green Conjure Bag and carry it with you.

KNOW that money is coming to you.

It may come from unexpected sources, but the finances do improve.

TO FULFILL ANY WISH

Remember - *keep it positive!*

Soak an uncut raw Moonstone in water along with a Quartz Crystal.

Do this three days prior to a new moon. When the time is up, take the Moonstone out and wear it on a chain. The chain needs to be long enough so that the Moonstone is at the same level as your Heart Chakra. Wear it constantly until the full moon. (You can remove it to bathe.)

When you first wear it, declare what you want.

Affirm: Nothing that is my Divine Right can be prevented in any way from being mine. I now attract (fill in your desire). It is done.

Then visualize what you desire.

Only use it for one purpose at a time. When you have the results, then you can use it again for a different desire.

TO REMOVE TENSION

Hold the stone named Turquoise in the hand you write with.

Close your eyes and visualize all your problems flowing into it.

Next, place it into a box and close the lid.

The next time you want to use the stone for any purpose, or carry it, remember to CLEANSE it first.

TO BRING IN COURAGE

(May also be utilized for strength.)

Wear a Bloodstone when you feel the situation might arise where you may need the qualities given.

LEADERSHIP ABILITY

To heighten your leadership qualities wear the Carnelian close to the base of your throat over your Throat Chakra.

This will also heighten your speaking ability.

Gives you protection from people who are jealous or do not wish you well.

MONEY ATTRACTION

Place Pyrite in your pocket, in your place of business, or home. The vibration of this gold colored stone will work after seven days. It is also known as Fools Gold.

SUCCESS

Anoint a Ruby with two drops of Success Oil.

Carry it with you at all times or wear it as jewelry.

Success will manifest to you.

SPIRITUALITY

Have the Lapis Lazuli close to you.

Heightens your Spirituality. Tunes you into Spirit. Heightens your intuitive level.

One of the main stones utilized by occultists.

HEALTH

Jasper is the strongest healing stone. Wear it to tone down pain and negative effects.

Use it to speed up your normal healing process.

TO NOT BE CONTROLLED

Wear Jasper at all times or carry it.

It will help you as it does not allow others to control you.

Aids in not letting others dominate you. Their hold over you will be lessened.

HIGH LUCK

The American Indians use this versatile Turquoise stone frequently.

It attracts luck when carried. Opens opportunities.

The luck may come in numerous forms such as: job offer, raise, promotion, lottery, new friends, positive love relationship, a problem solved.

PROTECTION

Wear the Fairy Cross or carry it in your wallet.

Formed by nature in the shape of a cross, no two are identical. They are mined in this form.

It gives protection on various levels such as against accidents and negative energy.

Also heightens your joy and love (which isn't too bad for fallout effects. You will simply have to put up with it.)

INTELLECT

When you study or you are gaining knowledge, use the Tiger Eye. It elevates your learning ability. You will learn faster and retain knowledge longer.

Here is an example: I explained this as one of the uses for the Tiger Eye to Larry, a business man.

Frequently, Larry was not able to retain all the information put forth at his company board meetings. His intellect was high; however, there was more information given at a fast pace in a short time span than he could absorb and remember.

Not really expecting this stone to aid very much, he tried it anyway, his theory being that it could not hurt.

Larry carried the stone in his wallet. After a short time he noticed that at each meeting his retention had improved greatly. With this knowledge came more self-confidence. Thus, between the vibration of the stone and his increased self-esteem, Larry was promoted rapidly.

DREAMS

To prevent bad dreams, place a Quartz Crystal under your pillow (or bed).

This can also be used to aid in heightening your dreams. Keep a pen and paper near your bed. As soon as you awake, write your dream down. Look at it later to see if there is information you should utilize, such as receiving numbers (lottery or other purpose) or ways to prevent a mistake you would have made.

In Australia the belief is that the information comes from the Wallaby, a spirit who communicates in dreams on a positive level.

HARMONY

To promote peace and harmony in your home, place a Sapphire in the room. It may appear to be a decoration to others. (It may also be placed out of sight if you wish.)

Do not have it enclosed - you don't want the vibrations to be closed in.

People may still argue. We are not controlling them. But they will argue less or simply go somewhere else.

WEATHER MAGIC

Control, utilized for a purpose, such as rain for crops on a farm. Not to be used lightly since nature has its own balance.

Use a terminated Quartz Crystal at the end of a Power Rod. Focus all your energy of White Light into the Rod. When you are ready, aim the rod at the clouds and visualize the energy force hitting it and the resulting rain.

The Druids had the ability for weather magic in various forms and could form clouds and rain with numerous other results.

They believed it was natural to have this ability since man is a part of nature and thus we are all connected.

ENERGY

Carry the stone called Beryl. It helps to overcome laziness, thus heightening your energy level.

When used as a rounded stone and exposed to the sun, it will light a fire.

SINCERITY

Give a Garnet to a person as a gift. When the person wears it, sincere qualities will be brought forth.

You can wear it to heighten your own level of sincerity.

RELIEVE DEPRESSION

Carry the Bloodstone at all times.

Affirm: God always takes care of me.
I leave all my problems in His hands.
He never fails me.
It is done.

Then walk with confidence. As you asked, He took over your problems, so you no longer need to dwell on them.

Carry the stone until the results come in.

LOVE

Wear a Rhodochrosite. It is one of the strongest stones for attracting love.

Anoint it with Love Oil or Patchouli Oil to raise the vibrational level even higher.

Wear it where it will be seen such as on a necklace.

MONEY DRAWING

Light a green candle measuring about seven inches in height. Hold a piece of Jasper in your passive hand. (The one you do not write with.)

Concentrate on the money needed and more coming in.

Use this Invocation:

As the Light in front of me,
I also have Divine Power shining through me.
As everything comes from above,
So now money comes also, enough and to spare,
To this material level,
as the stone before comes into being from Divine Power.
Thank you, Lord.
So Be It.

Repeat this for five minutes at night for seven nights in a row.

* * * * *

The stones can be utilized as a Power source.

Utilized as a form of divination such as Rune Stones, they can be very accurate. The stones have numerous purposes as discussed.

Try carrying one kind of stone for two weeks. Be aware of the feelings you have. Note your energy level, your dream state. Be cognizant of your financial situation for the two weeks.

The following two weeks carry a different stone and write down the results you noticed. Do this with as many different stones as you wish, keeping a record each time of the results.

Each will have a different vibration. Utilize them with your own vibrations.

CHAPTER TEN

PRAYER

Occult Grimoire & Magical Formulary A Workbook For Creating A Positive Life

PRAYER

THE ULTIMATE SOLUTION TO ALL LIFE'S PROBLEMS

The power of prayer is the strongest weapon we have. Look back at your life as a child. You will notice that what you wanted or needed came in. Not always as fast as you would have like, but it did come in.

Think of God as a big ball of White Light. This is the easiest way to explain it. Next, think of numerous beams of White Light, such as laser beams, coming from this ball. At the end of each beam is a smaller ball or spark of White Light. Each spark of Light is a person, a soul.

We are all directly connected to the Godhead. We are all part of Him. We are co-creators of our world, our reality.

With all this power, we can make anything happen in our lives. We can attract positive or negative situations.

Whatever thought we put power behind, we will make manifest. On a protection level, it is the strongest force known. Even if you do not know any form of psychic protection, prayer alone will protect you. You can use a known prayer, such as "The Lord's Prayer", or make up your own. They are all effective as long as you mean it from the heart, and have faith in the God Power. If you ask to be protected, He will do so. You will be one hundred percent taken care of. God does not make mistakes. Many cultures are aware of this and put it to practical every day use.

It does not matter if you all Him God, Buddha, Father Sky or whoever you have your Faith in. Whatever name is used, it stands for the One Source we all tune into.

Prayers come in various forms. Poetry is well known; verse; Psalms; talking to God. Any form you feel comfortable with will work.

We feel a close connection. It doesn't matter if you are speaking to Him on the level of "Thou Art...", "What It Be...", or "By the way...", - talking to God is talking to God. The point is to do it with sincerity. Then you will be heard.

There are numerous cultural approaches. American Indians think of Him as the Great Spirit, Father Sky or God. They have a very strong connection to nature, to nature spirits. They have a great respect for Mother Earth and know we are all connected. American Indians work in harmony, balance and respect with the forces of nature and God. They have a saying, "May The Great Spirit Watch Over You", which correlates to "May God Be With You". We all have the same connection.

In Hungary they believe in the "Isten" which means God. Everywhere on our planet are cultures with a belief in a Higher Being.

There are ways to utilize prayer to attract or repel. One of the strongest forces is the Psalms.

PSALMS

TO COME TO YOU

Example: Use when you have not heard from a person in a long time and want to be sure the person is well. It is meant as a last resort if there isn't any other way of contact. To be used only in a positive manner.

Read Psalm #92 - (King James Version) all the way through.

Then Psalm #35 - all the way through.

Psalm #103 - all the way through. Then go back and read Psalm #92 again. This time, after each verse call out the woman's (or man's) name that you want.

At the end of the Psalm, walk to a door or window facing East in your home. Open it a little and call the Name nine times, saying, "Wherever you are, whatever you are doing, you will have no peace, contentment or joy until you come to me". (Or "call me".) Only used for positive intent. Works in three days.

I used the Psalms as above when I lost touch with a friend for about a year. Ken was in the Army and it was hard to keep track of where he was at any given time.

He hadn't called for a while and I wanted to see how he was and touch base, so I prayed the Psalms. The answer always comes in within three days. However, he called on the fifth day. I didn't know what happened to him since it never takes so long.

He said he was in an airport trying to catch a flight. He was calling from Alaska and said he had had this urge to call me for days, but wasn't near a phone and couldn't get to one when this urge of his began. It took more than three days, but for a good reason.

FOR HELP

Pray Psalm #86 and concentrate on the area in which you need the help. Know that the help is coming in.

PRAYER FOR HELP

Pray Psalm #70. Concentrate on the help and on the people that wish you harm. Bless them and send love and healing energy.

FOR LEGAL MATTERS

Pray Psalm #74. Place some of the herb known as St. Johnworth in the hem of your clothes. Go to the river every day for three days prior to going to court, signing legal papers, etc.

TO PROTECT YOUR HOME

Write Verse two of Psalm #18 on parchment paper. Place this above the doorway of your front and back door. Keeps burglars away and/or incapable of entering.

Occult Grimoire & Magical Formulary A Workbook For Creating A Positive Life

OVERCOME ENEMIES

Write Verses six and seven of Psalm #80 on parchment paper. Concentrate on what you want. Then burn it and scatter to the wind outside your door.

BUSINESS TO GROW

Pray Psalm #115 every morning before going to work, and every night right before bed.

PROTECTION FROM PEOPLE WHO MEAN YOU HARM

Pray Psalm #64 and know you are protected by Divine Power. Bless those who are your enemies and send them on their way.

WHEN YOU ARE DEPRESSED

Pray Psalm #86 from your heart.

THANKS FOR PRAYERS ANSWERED

Pray Psalm #66 with joy and happiness. After all, you have been answered.

PSYCHIC ABILITY STRENGTHENED

Write Verses one and four of Psalm #49 on parchment paper. Place this under a brown candle. Burn the candle when you practice any psychic ability.

SPIRITUALITY

Pray Psalm #46 when required.

TO BE SAFE DURING TRAVEL

Write Verses six and seven of Psalm #28 on parchment paper. Wrap this in a handkerchief and carry in your pocket on the journey.

LOVE ATTRACTION

Pray Psalm #67 once each week (Friday being the best day). Write it on parchment paper, anoint the edges with Attraction Oil once a week. Start from the top left corner and go towards the right top corner. Carry this in your pocket when leaving your home.

WHEN FACED WITH PROBLEMS

Pray Psalm #70 sincerely. Then say, "Thank you, Father". When you ask, He will deliver help.

LOVE

Pray Psalm #47 each morning. Remember to be happy and to show love to everyone. What you send out, you get back.

INCREASE OF CROPS

Pray Psalm #67. Repeat Verses five, six and seven again. Listen to your intuition on how to handle situations. Do this every morning and before bed every night. You may receive direction during your dream state.

DELIVERANCE FROM PERSECUTORS

Pray Psalm #142 each day and walk in the Path of the Lord.

TO BE BLESSED

Pray Psalm #41 and live in the Path of the Light. Burn a white on a purple candle.

FOR A HARMONIOUS FAMILY

Pray Psalm #128 every night and burn a yellow candle simultaneously.

MONEY ATTRACTION

Pray Psalm #72. Follow your hunches and also work on a realistic level on this plane.

LUCK

Pray Psalm #65 once a week and burn a purple candle at the same time. You also need to deal on an ethical level, work hard and be open to opportunities.

PROTECTION FROM ENEMIES

Pray Psalm #100. You cannot overdo the Prayer.

PETITION

Pray Psalm #141. On one side of parchment paper write your petition. On the other side, write Verse one and two of Psalm #141. Put this in an incense burner.

Place Helping Hand or Coconut Incense on top of it. Burn these every day until the prayer is answered. Redo until the answer comes.

TURN YOUR LUCK AROUND

Pray Psalm #62 and burn the Uncrossing Incense or Coconut Incense each day.

TO PRAISE GOD

Pray Psalm #92 and give thanks for all you have received in your lifetime.

HELP IN TIMES OF TROUBLE

Pray Psalm #11 and concentrate on the meaning of the words. Know that He will help you.

BRING US JOY

Pray Psalm #126. Spend a few minutes on the meaning of this Psalm and let there be joy in your heart.

CLEARING OF CONFUSION

Pray Psalm #115. Repeat Verses nine, ten and eleven. Do this with conviction and trust.

LOVE ATTRACTIONS

Pray Psalm #111. Repeat Verses four every morning. Remember to be positive and sincere with others. Radiate the joy and the warmth of the God Light within you.

ATTRACT GOOD BUSINESS

Pray Psalm #8 each morning before work. Write it on parchment paper and place it at your place of business. (By the phone, in your desk, cash box, etc.) Remember Verse five. How can we fail?

WISDOM

Pray Verses 97 to 104 of Psalm #119. Do this often to increase knowledge and wisdom coming in to you.

TO BRING IN HELP WHEN NEEDED

Pray Psalm #40. Do this twice with faith in your heart.

TO FOCUS ON A POSITIVE FUTURE

Read Psalm #117. Do this each morning and each night.

AFFIRMATIONS

Affirmations are a form of prayer. They are positive statements. They manifest what you want into your life.

The affirmation in essence states everything in the NOW. (I am, I have, I do.) It is an assumption in some affirmations that you are able to manifest your needs *only* because you do so through God. In other affirmations this assumption is more obvious and clearly stated.

This is a way to speak to God and let Him know your needs. You are putting it in the present tense knowing that what you ask of God is already answered. Thus, the affirmation is in statement form.

What we think, we can manifest. If we do not like what has been manifested into our lives, we change the thought and manifest something else. As co-creators we are responsible for our lives and the paths they take.

Take note of what you say most often. Is it, "I never have a good job", or "I always have a job I love"? You will find it manifesting in your life. Do you say, "Nothing good ever happens to me"? As long as you believe this, it will keep manifesting for you. You need to change your thinking to saying, "Good things always happen to me". Then they will!

All creation is perfect. The Universal Law is always in motion. If you look at the world around you, it will reinforce this knowledge. Look at nature and how it all moves in its own patterns. So do we.

Some of us move faster, some at different levels and varied experiences. We all are working on our Paths.

If you are on a negative Path or in a direction you do not wish to go, you have the POWER to change it. We all have free will.

First you need to decide what you wish to change, or want, then work towards it.

Some of your outlook will be from your own experiences. Some will be from your parents and the people you associated with. You may have picked up their outlook. You may have been told repeatedly that you would never accomplish anything and after years of listening, you started to really believe it.

Do not believe in limitations. God never puts one on us. So why should we?

What we think about will manifest. The Universal Law gives us whatever we ask for, good or bad. It is neutral and does not question whether or not we really want what we repeatedly think. It simply delivers.

Many people are not aware of this past conditioning. Others may have been told such things as, "You cannot handle bills", or "You are not smart enough to...". Past conditioning is what puts you at this point in your life at this particular time.

Do not feel bad if you are not at the point you want to be. It hasn't been your fault. However, knowing this now, you have to make the decisions of where you want to be tomorrow and in the future. Then work on it. There is nothing holding you back but yourself.

Jesus said, "And all things, whatsoever ye shall ask in prayer, believing, ye shall receive". (Matt. 21:22) *and*

"Therefore I say unto you, what things soever ye desire, when ye pray, believe that ye receive them, and ye shall have them". (Mark 11:24)

Act as though you already have it. Remember that faith without action is dead, so help it along on this reality also.

Do not scatter your forces by telling others of your problems, of things that do not go well for you. Remember the saying, "Silence is golden", and act accordingly. You want all your focus on the positive.

When things are not coming into your life as you need, say the following, "The walls of lack and delay now crumble away, and I enter my Promised Land, Under Grace."

Visualize the Walls of Jericho crumbling as you affirm this. Then see yourself stepping over it to the other side easily and with joy.

Material things are easy to manifest. Trust God for your supply of all your needs. Things (possessions, money) are God being manifested.

"What Allah has given cannot be diminished."

There is a saying that when one door shuts, another one opens.

Visualize the things that seem out of reach to you. Expect them NOW, through Divine Power, in unexpected ways. God does work in mysterious (unexpected) ways.

"I now catch up with my good, for before I called, I was answered."

OCCULT LAW OF INDIFFERENCE

None of these things disturb me.

It means you should not want things too intensely. If you do, you will cancel it out. Simply know that it is coming in.

When you have tried and there is nothing left to try on our working level, turn to God and leave it all to Him. Do not try to figure out how things will be solved. Just trust and say, "I let God juggle the situation."

The Law of Grace is the only power that will cancel out Karma. Example: If in a previous life, or in this one, you mishandled money, there is still time to change things. You need to understand how to deal with money in a positive way. Acknowledge it to God in a prayer. If you really understand and mean it from the heart when you say you will work with it, on a positive level, your negative Karma will be canceled.

Make all your demands of the Universal Supply. Ask for your needs by *Divine Right* (God made the promise to us), through *Divine Power* (where everything comes from) and *In a Perfect Way* (we do not want to harm anyone).

Your Power to Manifest is always in the present time. What you wanted or thought five years ago or more is manifesting. That is over with, but you can still control your future. Your thoughts can be changed to positive. It is a matter of reconditioning yourself.

Notice more frequently what you reaffirm in your thoughts. Take note of the thoughts that keep coming in. At work do you say, "This is too hard", or "I can't do this"? In other situations, do you make statements like, "I never have a good relationship", or "I always mess up"? In making such statements you actually keep those situations coming in. Turn the words around to make them positive.

The more we lack self-confidence and love of ourselves, the more we are bound to attract negative situations. We cannot help the patterns from the past - we are all human. To change these patterns you need to affirm that you have confidence in yourself and love yourself. You have to care about yourself before others can. We all feel we are not good enough.

Write a list of all the things you feel are negative concerning yourself. We all have these or similar ideas about ourselves.

I am too tall.	I am not smart enough.
I never get what I want.	Nobody cares about me.
I do not deserve money.	I am ugly.
I do not deserve to be loved.	I am not healthy
Nobody recognizes what I do for them.	

Then look at your list. What do you feel? What is coming from what others (parents, teachers, etc.) are telling? Change your thought and remove these conditions.

You need to say the affirmation to yourself as often as possible. You may feel funny at first; but you can't overdo it, and who will know what you are thinking anyway?

AFFIRMATIONS TO COUNTERACT

NEGATIVE THOUGHT RESULTS PATTERN	TO MANIFEST POSITIVE
I cannot move.	I move to the Perfect affordable home for me NOW.
I hate my job.	I love my job and get along with everyone.
I do not make enough money.	Money flows easily and abundantly to me.
I always need money.	My supply is God. As money goes out, it comes back immediately. My wallet is always full under Grace, in a Perfect Way.
It is too difficult for me.	God clears the way where there isn't one, Through Grace, in a Perfect Way.

I am never fortunate.	Now is the time of my appointed good fortune.
I never make the right decision.	I am divinely led and listen to my intuition. I go forward easily.
I am always unlucky.	God flows through me. I am luck incarnated.
My life is terrible.	I am willing to release the negative pattern that caused this. I now have a prosperous, happy life.
Nothing goes right for me.	I deserve the best and accept it NOW.
I am... (negative habit, drink, smoke, eat too much, etc.)	I am safe and God takes care of me.
I am lonely.	I am loved and loving.
I do not have a good relationship.	I have a perfect, loving relationship.
I can never do well on	I manifest a new and better job NOW.

this job.

I have problems with landlords.	My landlord works with me easily and easily and happily. All goes well.
I do not have money for a new car.	I have my Perfect, affordable car. It comes in easily.
I am afraid.	I am safe. It is safe to be myself. My Father takes care of me.
I cannot handle all these bills.	The Universal Bank is always abundant. It supplies all my needs and more.
I can never afford a nice suit. (dress, etc.)	I deserve the best. It comes to me easily.
I never have anything.	All my needs are met. (Recognize them as they come in. It may be through money, as a gift, or the possession itself.)
I do not have success.	What God does for others, He now does for me and more, in a Perfect Way.

I am so scattered.	I am well organized. I enjoy and have fun with it.
I am always sick.	I am healthy and feel safe.
I always get lost.	God guides me and I am never lost.
It is hard to sell my old car.	I sell my car quickly and profitably.
I am always tired.	I am full of the energy of life. I enjoy life to the fullest.
I am confused.	I make decisions easily and readily. God guides me.
I do not know why this happened to me.	I only attract positive situations into my life.
Trouble always follows me.	Everything comes easily, freely and happily to me.
I can't do...	God and I are One. Therefore I can do everything.

I always have negative, happily unfriendly people at my work.	I always work well and with my boss and co-workers.
I do not have enough money.	My supply comes from God. My magic wallet is always overflowing.

Next, you visualize yourself already in the new positive situation. You will see how it comes in just the way you are putting the thought out.

Remember that where you are now does not matter. Do not look back. You cannot change the past. Look at the future and decide now what you want in it.

Do not try to change others. We can only change ourselves. As you become more positive you may notice your negative friends leaving your life.

Now this is not negative. It does not mean they should not have been in your life. There was a valid reason at the time but you have now outgrown them. Bless them and let them go. New people who are more positive will be attracted to you. This is how it should be. You are growing in your God Consciousness.

Never let other people make you feel guilty. Do not accept it. When they try, look at what they are saying. Is it true?

As an example: You had agreed to give a friend a ride in your car somewhere and you were late due to the car breaking down. You tried your best, you apologized and explained why you were late. How bad can you really feel when it wasn't under your control? It is not as though you forgot or did not bother to get up in time. So, forgive yourself and do not accept the guilt. You did your best.

Whenever anything negative is said to you, first ask yourself, "Is this true about me"? If it is, then work on it. If not, reject it. Just say to yourself, "I cancel this thought". Or reword it to a positive thought.

PROTECTION PRAYER

In ancient times, prayers were used as protection. Some of these are in verse form. One such prayer was used to visualize a dome of the White Light of God to cover a person while asleep and unable to protect themselves. This was used by the adepts.

It has been passed down, and in so doing, the purpose on this higher level was lost. It is still in use to this day, albeit it is now considered a children's night time prayer.

Learn the prayer and use it with the visualization of the White Dome of Light covering the bed and surrounding it.

Repeat the following prayer:

There are four corners on my bed,

There are four angels at the head,

Matthew, Mark, Luke and John,

Please Bless this bed that I lay on.

Amen.

Another prayer:

God protect me through the night,
Through the negative energies that try to bind,
In the name of the Father, the Son and the Holy Spirit,
Let the White Light of God enfold me within it.
Amen
I am One with the force of Divine Power,
I am One with the Universal Mind,
I am protected on all the astral levels,
When I walk with my hand in God's
Amen.

Guide me in the direction You choose,
For I trust in your protection.
I am One with the Power that created me,
And know I am taken care of.
Amen.

Help me learn to listen within,
To experience success, health and joy.
Help me to understand You better.
God protect me from evil doers.
Amen.

WISHES FULFILLED

Write a letter to God as a prayer. Use white paper. Make it in a letter form. Write as follows:

Dear God,

    Please hear my prayer. I need (fill in whatever your needs are). I need this now.

    I trust in you and know that as I ask, it is already set in motion, and my prayer is answered.

    Thank you, Father.

                     Love,
                     (sign your name)

Next, take the letter and place it between the pages of your Bible. Do not tell anyone until after you are answered. You do not need anyone sending negative energy to negate it. Leave it in the Bible until it comes to pass. Remember to thank God when it comes in.

YOUR OWN PRAYER

You can make up your own prayer. You need to cover certain areas. Always ask only on a *positive* level.

Add a word representing the present such as: *now, immediately.* Visualize the outcome.

Remember Aladdin's lamp? Anything he wished for, he could have with the help of the genie.

You have something better than Aladdin - you ask God or work with Spirit and as you ask, it is already worked on; done.

You have the power to create whatever you need. Start with whatever your priority is, NOW.

CONCLUSION

Being part of God, we are meant to be happy. We have the Divine Spark within us. We are given the insight and tools to do so. We are the ones who decide what Path we will take.

Remember the Indwelling God when doing Spiritual work. As in Psalm #62, "My soul, wait thou only upon God; for my expectation is from Him."

Only work on a positive level to receive the full benefit of working in the Light. Working for yourself or others, the Power will be full force.

As you pass the positive knowledge on to others, you will help to make this a better world. I think of it this way: As each person that I help becomes in tune with his/her inner self, that person glows within the White Light. One by one, I am helping to Light up the World - and so can you.

Use the knowledge in this book to aid you to better your life. As a Mystic, I find this ancient knowledge needs to be passed on and put to proper use.

Go forth as Light Workers with a positive attitude and the knowledge that God dwells within each of us. We are all connected with each other and with nature through the White Light.

Through understanding yourself, you will become in tune with nature.

QUIZ

1. You need to close your aura after you meditate.
   T___ F___

2. Our normal everyday thoughts are on a Theta level.
   T___ F___

3. You use infusion with a talisman.
   T___ F___

4. When in a dream state, you can't tune into prophetic information.
   T___ F___

5. The sloe berry is used in love potions.
   T___ F___

6. It doesn't make a difference what your thoughts are since nobody else will know.
   T___ F___

7. When Treasure Mapping, you should tell everyone about it so they can send positive energy to help.
   T___ F___

8. You can place a symbol of God on your Treasure Map but it is not important to do so.
   T___ F___

9. For prayer to work, you need to pray sincerely.

T___ F___

10. Prayer can help in every situation.

    T___ F___

11. If you do not use the word "God", prayer will not work.

    T___ F___

12. We all feel we deserve the best.

    T___ F___

13. You have to love yourself before others can love you.

    T___ F___

14. Our childhood experiences no longer affect us.

    T___ F___

15. Thoughts create everything in our lives.

    T___ F___

16. Negative thought patterns can be changed.

    T___ F___

17. We are all One with God and are co-creators.

    T___ F___

18. Health is not changeable through thought.

    T___ F___

19. It is more difficult to attract money than anything else.

    T___ F___

20. We always receive what we put out.

    T___ F___

21. When you work with manifesting through Divine Power, you no longer need to go out of your way to help bring it in.

    T___ F___

22. Universal Law always supplies what you ask for.

    T___ F___

23. Only some people have chi.

    T___ F___

24. We can choose not to accept guilt from others.

    T___ F___

25. All your wishes can be fulfilled.

    T___ F___

26. Prayers of protection are only used by adults.

    T___ F___

27. When you put your Shield of Protection up, it keeps all energy out - negative and positive.

    T___ F___

28. Quartz crystals need to be terminated - coming to a point - to be utilized for protection.

    T___ F___

29. Psychic self-defense only protects us from spirits.

    T___ F___

30. You are attacked in your aura.

    T___ F___

31. Spiritual baths have their own vibrations.

    T___ F___

32. The strongest psychic defense is the Shield of Protection and Prayer.

    T___ F___

33. You can use the shield only for yourself.

Occult Grimoire & Magical Formulary A Workbook For Creating A Positive Life

T___ F___

34. Candles are only used for magical purposes.

    T___ F___

35. You can use the same candle for two different "works" if you have not finished it when you are done with the first.

    T___ F___

36. Incense is used only at specific times.

    T___ F___

37. Incense only comes in stick and cone form.

    T___ F___

38. The Bible contains references to the use of incense in numerous places.

    T___ F___

39. 7 African Powers incense refers to the 7 deities in VooDoo.

    T___ F___

40. The red candle is used to attract love.

    T___ F___

41. Incense is only used by occult practitioners.

    T___ F___

42. The powder and stick incense burn exactly the same amount of time.

    T___ F___

43. Cutting an oil gives it more power.

    T___ F___

44. Success oil is only for business gain.

    T___ F___

45. Meditation can be heightened by a stone.

    T___ F___

46. Merlin is said to have utilized the quartz crystal.

    T___ F___

47. Amethyst is said to help prevent being drunk.

    T___ F___

48. Quartz crystals can aid in weather control.

    T___ F___

49. The Fairy Cross is shaped by man in a cross form.

    T___ F___

50. All our abilities come from Divine Power.

    T___ F___

1.	True	26.	False
2.	False	27.	False
3.	False	28.	False
4.	False	29.	False
5.	True	30.	True
6.	False	31.	True
7.	False	32.	True
8.	False	33.	False
9.	True	34.	False
10.	True	35.	False
11.	False	36.	False
12.	False	37.	False
13.	True	38.	True
14.	False	39.	True
15.	True	40.	True
16.	True	41.	False
17.	True	42.	False
18.	False	43.	False
19.	False	44.	False
20.	False	45.	True
21.	False	46.	True
22.	True	47.	True
23.	False	48.	True
24.	True	49.	False
25.	True	50.	True

GLOSSARY

ADEPT: Person who is working on the Highest level applying his knowledge of Universal Law to living. Has the control over himself and Universal Forces.

AFFIRMATION: Statement. Positive remark in a sentence.

CHAKRA: A Sanskrit word. It is a whirling energy vortex center. The energy centers run along your spine from the base to above your head. Some psychics clairvoyantly "see" this. Each Chakra correlates to a different color, vibration and purpose. There are seven from the base going upward.

CHI: Named in China. In Japan called Ki. Primal energy. Vital life force. Utilizes the Power of thought and energy.

CONJURE BAG: A pouch which contains objects to attract what you want in your life, or to repel.

DEVA: Shining ones. Spirits.

DRUID: Celtic in origin. Mystics of the higher levels, such as shape-changing, working with nature spirits and the more advanced psychic abilities.

ELEGGUA: One of the most powerful African gods. He opens and closes all types of doors. You can also call Eleggua for protection of your home or self.

EVIL EYE: Said to be a stare which can cause great harm or evil to the one looked upon.

INCANTATION: A chant with demand. Often repeated and can also be with rhyme.

INFUSION: To let herbs soak in hot water to get the expected results, one teaspoon herb to one cup of water. Do not use metal pots. Keep the pot covered. Boil water and pour over the herb. Leave for five to fifteen minutes. Strain.

INVOCATION: Prayer or seriously addressing higher being (God).

KARMA: Law of action. For every action there is a reaction. What you set up in your life, good or bad, come back.

MACERATE: To make a solid substance soft by soaking in a liquid. To thin it out.

MAGI: Zoroastrian priests. Psychics who work with alchemy, astrology, control nature forces and supernatural abilities.

MAGIC: The utilization of psychic energy to make changes.

MANIFEST: To reveal. To bring forth.

MOJO BAG: Same as a Conjure Bag.

PROPHECY: A prediction.

PSYCHIC: A person who receives information without the use of the five senses.

SPELL: Ritual in magic to bring about a result you want.

TERMINATED CRYSTAL: A crystal with a point at one or both ends.

VISUALIZE: To consciously bring into manifestation a desire by an exercise of picturing the desire.

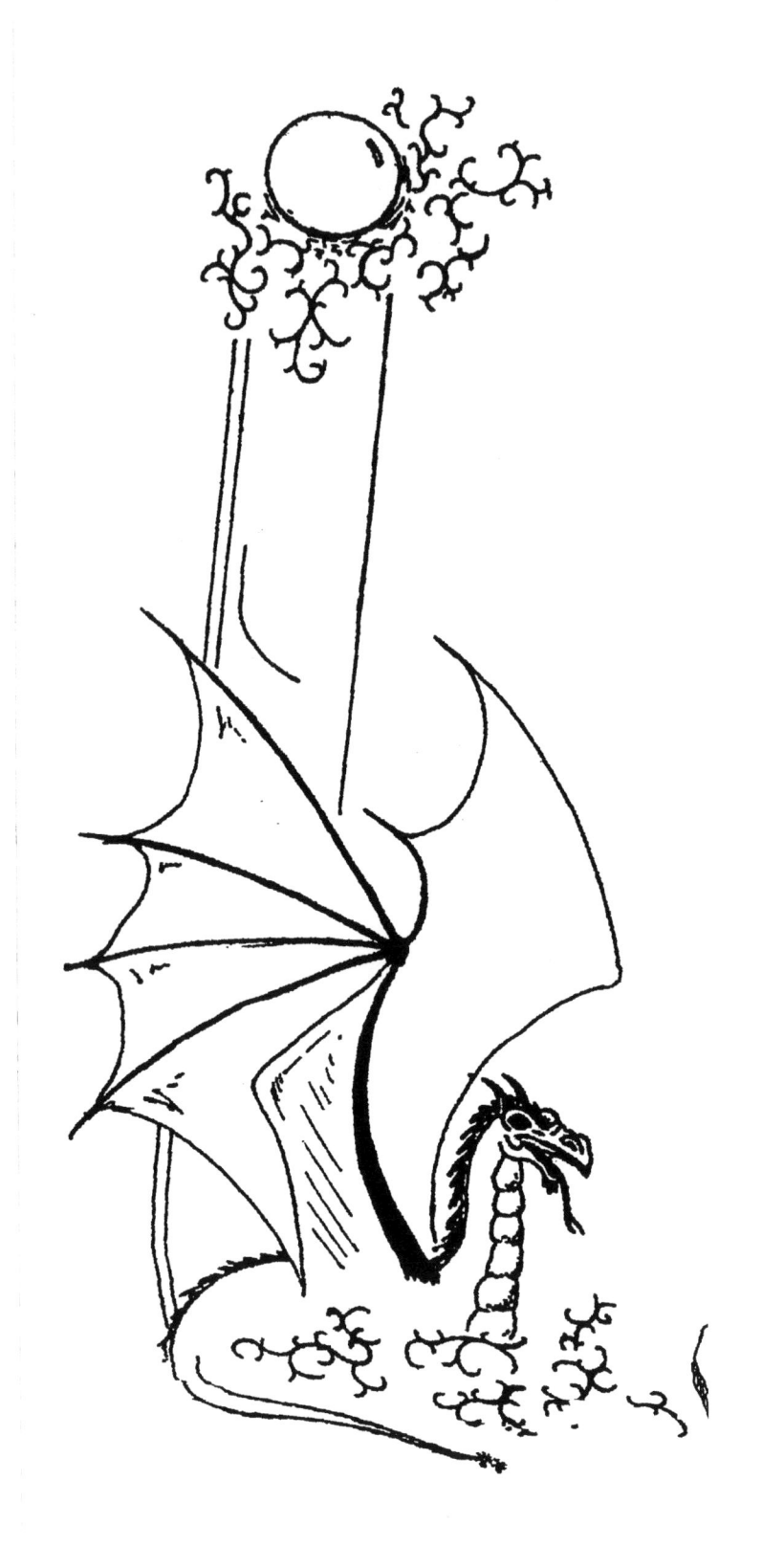

Occult Grimoire & Magical Formulary A Workbook For Creating A Positive Life

Prayer for Power

I am one with God
    and let the power of God
        flow in me,
            through me,
                and around me
For God is All.
    I trust the Divine Power
        and all is perfect,
Knowing I am always protected
    and guided Divinely.
Whatever I choose
    to manifest in my life
        comes easily to me,
Joyfully and with perfect harmony.
    I walk the path of White Light
        in Truth, Peace,
            Love,
            Harmony and Health.
Thank you, Father, for I am,
    You are,
        We are ONE.
            AMEN.

by Rev. Maria Solomon

ABOUT THE AUTHOR

Rev. Maria D'Andrea was born in Budapest, Hungary. Since early childhood, she has demonstrated a high degree of psychic ability. As an Ordained Minister and Pastoral Counselor, Maria has provided excellent psychic guidance and enlightenment to many.

Rev. Maria's psychic abilities and talents over the past years include: Rune Casting, Tarot Card Reading, Clairvoyance, Clairaudience, Empath, Clairsentience, Crystal Gazing, Palmistry, Biorhythm, Handwriting Analysis, Numerology, Trance States, Automatic Writing, Past Lives, Psychometry, Dowsing, Numberology, Chinese Er Mei Qi Gong, Occultism, Kirlian Photography, Pshychic Investigations, Personnel Screening, the teaching of Psychic and Metaphysical techniques, meditation principles and techniques. She is a Certified Hypnotherapist and holds a Doctor of Metaphysics degree (Ms.D.). She is also an Ambassador in Ministry, Principal Teacher in ISA and holds the titles of D.D. and D.R.H.

She has been a guest speaker at metaphysical and occult organizations throughout the United States. She has also published articles on spiritual and pastoral guidance in numerous magazines and professional journals and continues to do so today. Among her credits are numerous appearances on radio and television shows.

Rev. Maria is the founder of the Sylvan Society - a hermetic order, the founder of the "D'Andrea Institute of Esoteric Studies", a member of the Spiritual Frontier Fellowship, the Floating Healing Meditation Circle, the Life Study Fellowship, the Psychic Guild, A.R.E. (the Association for Research and Enlightenment), honorary member of the Tucscarora Indian Tribe, the Ghost Research Society and the Long Island School of Applied Hypnosis.

Rev. Maria D'Andrea can be reached through her web site.

www.mariadandrea.com

Occult Grimoire & Magical Formulary A Workbook For Creating A Positive Life

MARIA D' ANDREA'S YOUR PERSONAL MEGA POWER SPELLS
For Love, Luck, Prosperity
Self Empowerment Through Wicca & White Magick
By Maria D' Andrea

"PUT A SPELL ON YOU CAUSE YOU'RE MINE" Those are the words of the great bluesman Screamin' Jay Hawkins, who was years ahead of Alice Cooper, Black Sabbath and a multitude of Heavy Metal bands seeking to embrace - and sometimes exploit - a bit of the macabre in their musical persona, including various aspects of occultism, from "Satanism" to Voodoo to Hoodoo. As a rock enthusiast, I truly admire Screamin' Jay, for he was genuinely authentic and an original - no doubt reinforced by a real visit to the infamous "crossroads" sometime in his life.

Maria has been using certain aspects of witchcraft in a positive way for many years and she feels it is high time she share this information as well as the best spells of Wicca with you. Thus the work you now hold in your hands.

So take a deep breath and let us go and find the most powerful Mega Spells that will benefit our lives and make us more affirmative and spiritually positive individuals. It's to our uppermost advantage to do so.

$29.95 + $5.00 Shipping

I know of what I speak when I tell you she has always relied upon God's help for guidance and inspiration. Whether she is harnessing very traditional Christian sentimentalities or depending upon more paganistic stimulation, the gifted psychic always calls upon the Divine Creator for her most important inspirations.
~Timothy Green Beckley

This book is a Light Worker's guide to utilizing ancient tools for modern times. As well as my own proven secret formulae.

Information has been passed down by word of mouth from the ancient wise known by titles such as magis, shamans, priestesses, elders, vitkis and sages.

Throughout every age and culture, there have been genuine practitioners of our higher inner circles who continue to work only on the positive Path of Divine Light.

Know the Self first and your true connection to the Oneness with God.

Your source is always within yourself, not from outward.
$29.95 + $5.00 Shipping

HEAVEN SENT MONEY SPELLS
Divinely Inspired For Your Wealth
Maria D' Andrea

Occult Grimoire & Magical Formulary A Workbook For Creating A Positive Life

Global Communications, Box 753, New Brunswick, NJ 08903
Credit Card Orders 732 602-3407   MRUFO8@hotmail.com

OTHER BOOKS
BY MARIA D'ANDREA

Psychic Vibrations of Crystals, Gems and Stones
Instant Money Empowerment
ISBN# 0-942272-750-7
Helping Yourself With Magickal Oils A-Z
ISBN# 0-942272-49-8
Love and Light in the Garden of God - Collective Writings
Do It Yourself Wicca
How To Terminate Stress With Mediation Strategies

SERVICES & PRODUCTS

Numerous Classes, Guided Meditation,

Tapes, CDs, DVDs and products available

by writing directly to author.

FOR ADDITIONAL INFORMATION

Rev. Maria D'Andrea MsD, DRH, D.D.

The Sylvan Society
The Psi Esoteric Guild
The D'Andrea Institute of Esoteric Studies
www.mariadandrea.com

Occult Grimoire & Magical Formulary A Workbook For Creating A Positive Life

Maria Solomon famed Author & Occultist gives us a workbook for creating a positive life utilizing formulae and techniques that really work!

Ancient Direct & Simplified !!!

You will easily and Immediately learn how to :
Manifest your own future!
Prevent Psychic attack!
Use Candles, herbs and oils as "Power Magnets"!
Burn incense to achieve your goals!
Learn precisely how to use formulae, love potions, and herbal mixtures to get what you want out of life!

DOZENS OF REAL RECIPTES, FORMULAE AND TECHNIQUES THAT REALLY WORK !

Printed in Great Britain
by Amazon